Animal Doodle
WILDLIFE COLORING BOOK

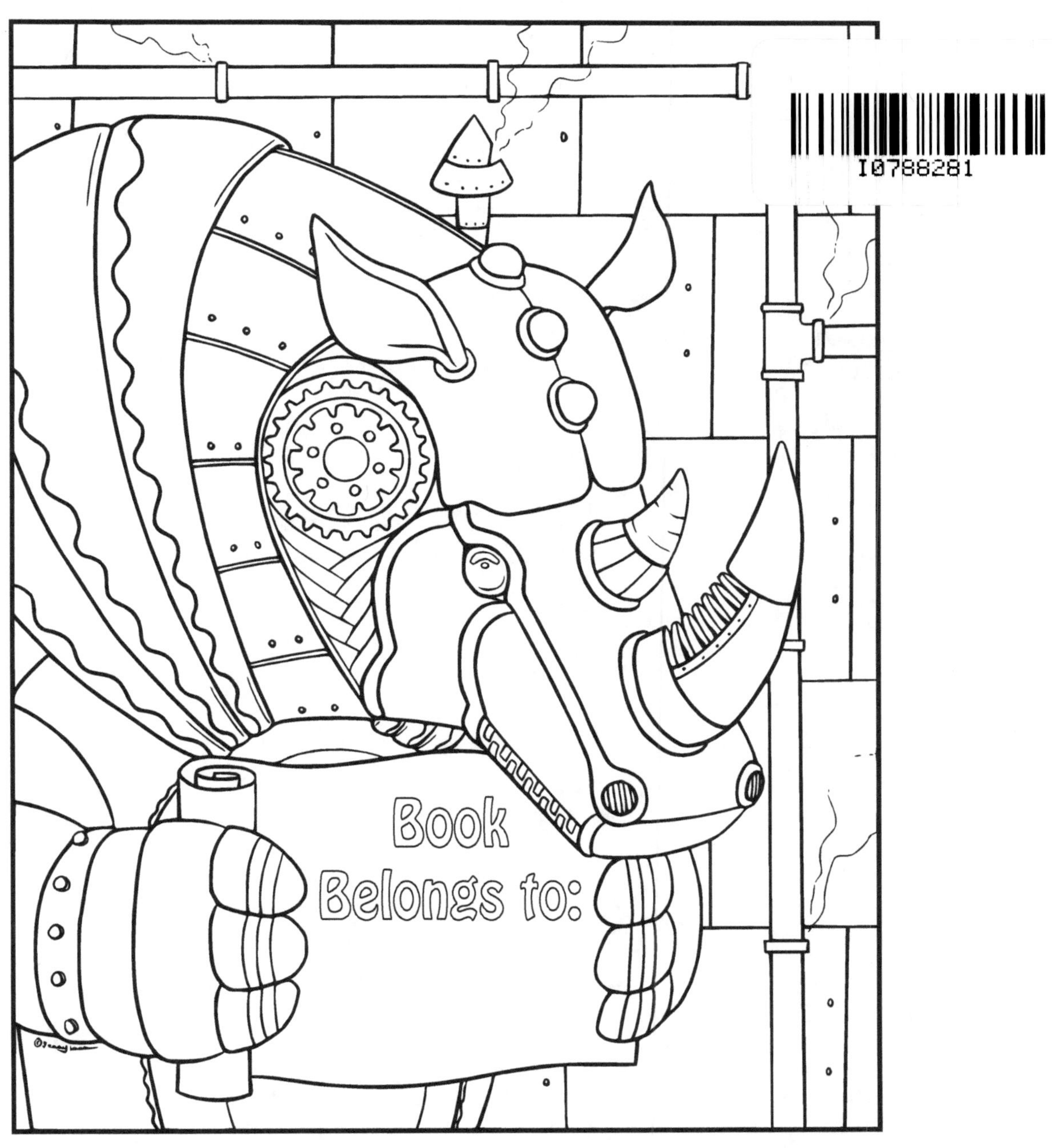

© BY JENNY LUAN

Animal Doodle
WILDLIFE COLORING BOOK

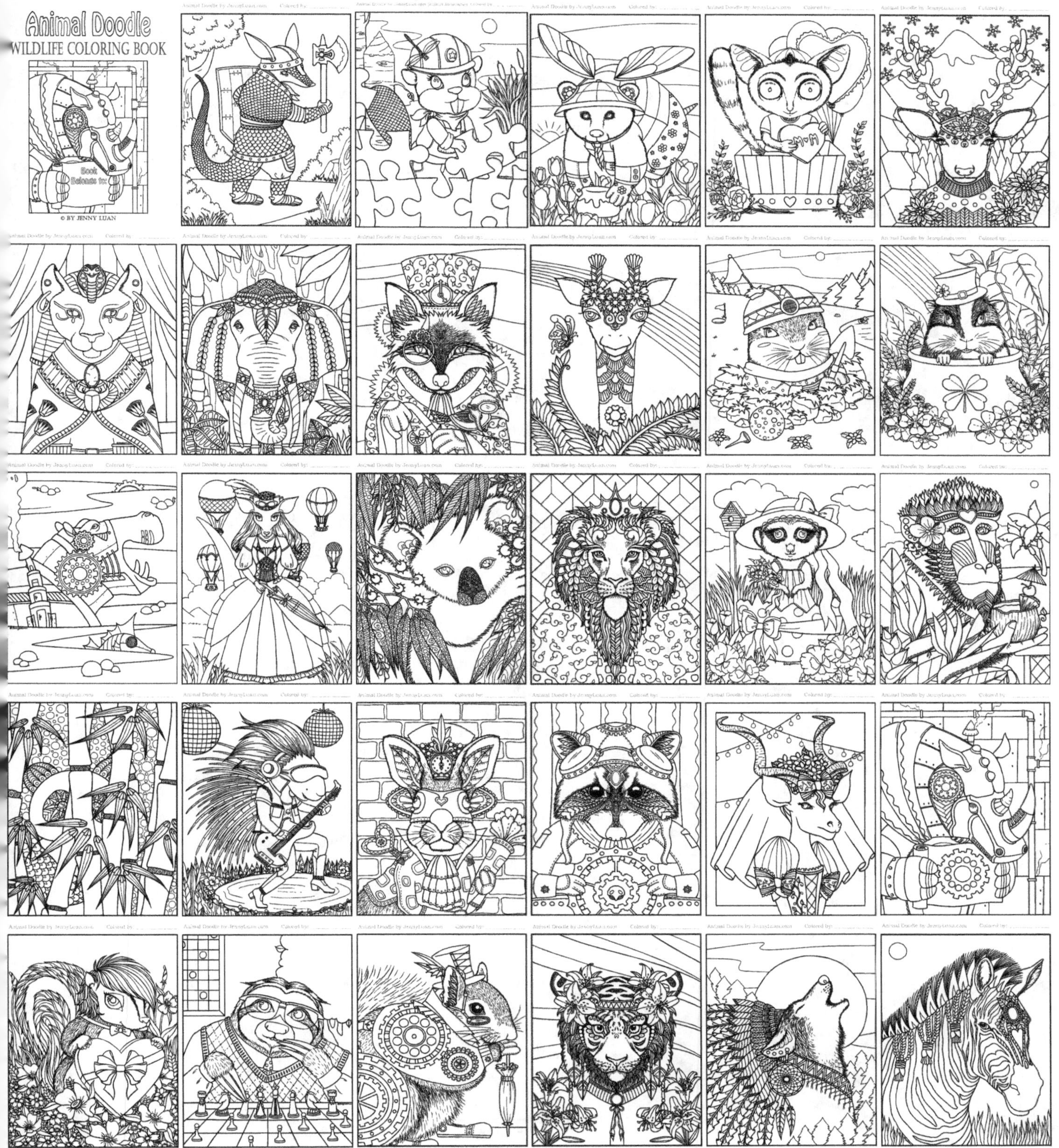

My Personal Favorite Coloring Tips

Colored Pencils:

How I color: I like to keep pencils sharp and use short strokes.

Water based: I use very little water with watercolor brushes.

Wax and oil based: I like to use odorless mineral spirits with a Q-tip or brush. Some people use Vaseline to blend.

Markers:

I would put a blotter paper or card stock in between each coloring page because most markers bleed through to the next page.

Water based: I use very little water with watercolor brush to blend.

Alcohol Based: I use their brand of blender markers.

India ink base: they are more light-fast but don't blend easily.

Permanent markers: I would put a blotter paper or card stock in between each coloring page because they will bleed through to the next page.

Gel Pen: I love to use glitter gel pens to add sparkles on my coloring. Gel pen work well in a small area.

Mix media tips:

Colored pencils can be used on top of markers for shading.

Glitter or metallic gel pens can lay well on top of markers.

Thank you for supporting independent artists. In order to create affordable books, I use Amazon's Create Space on Demand publishing. Create Space only offers one paper weight with no perforated pages option. I want to make sure you are aware of their limitation because I have no choice in the matter and I value your positive feedback. Please contact me if you have questions about my books.

JennyLuan.com

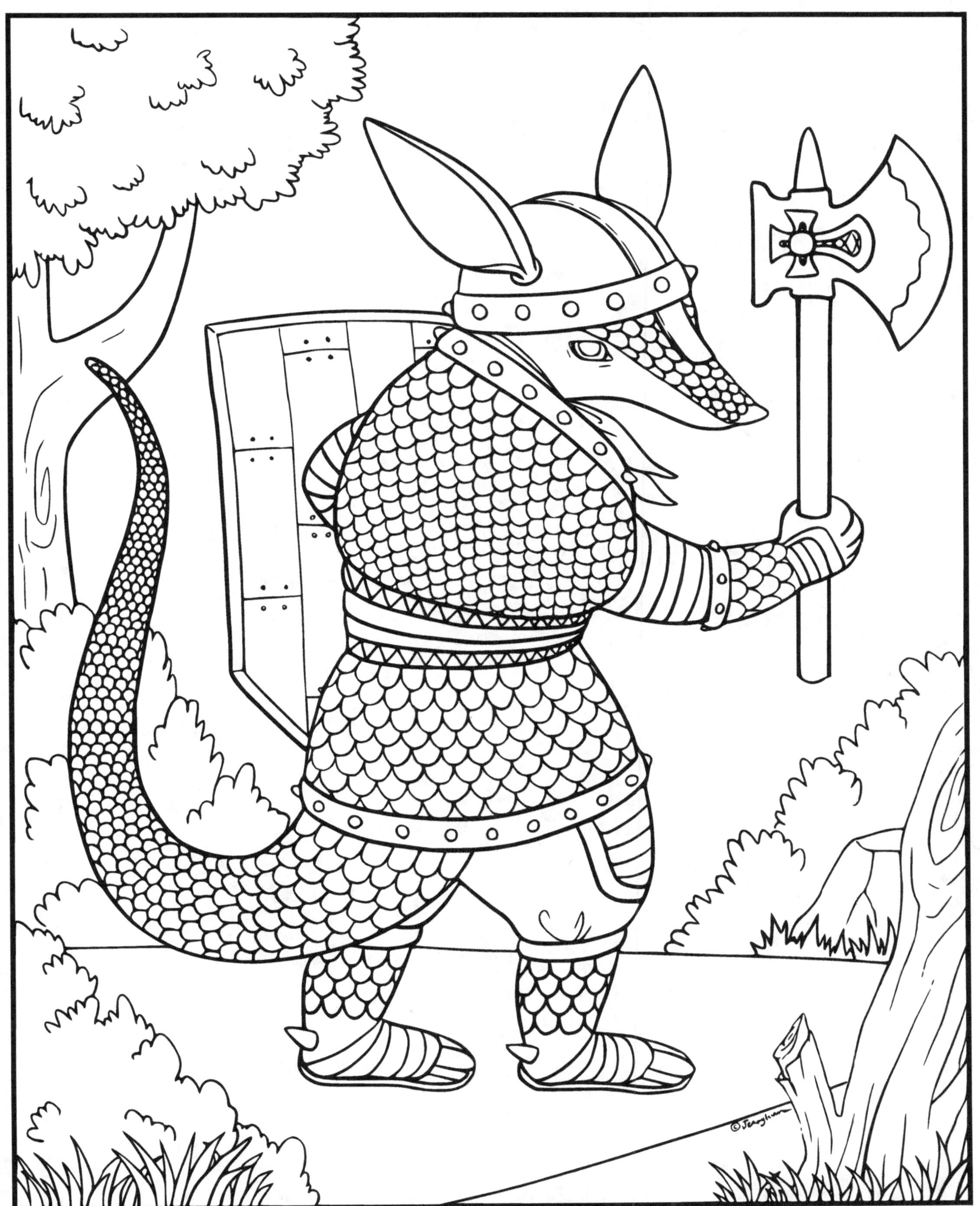

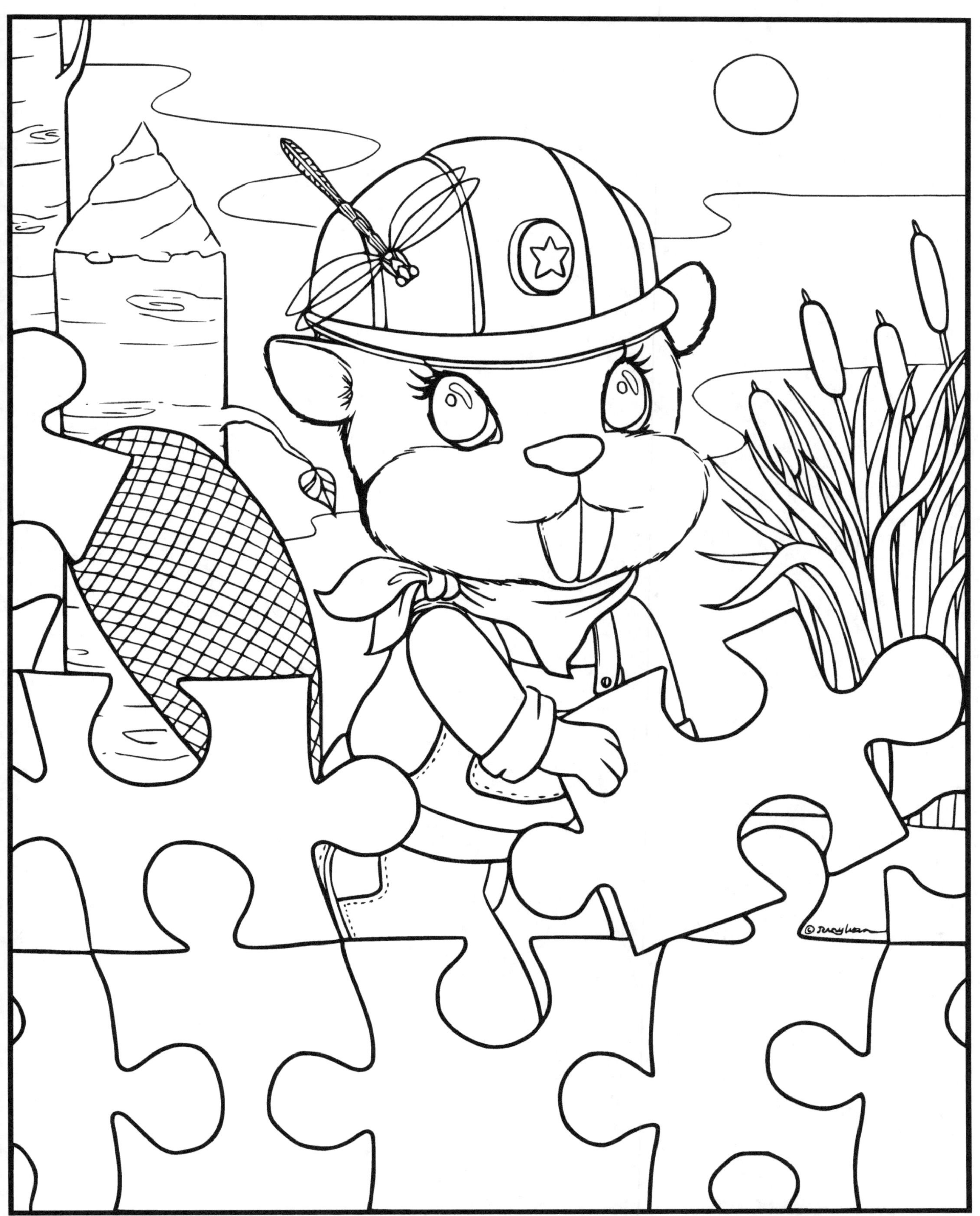

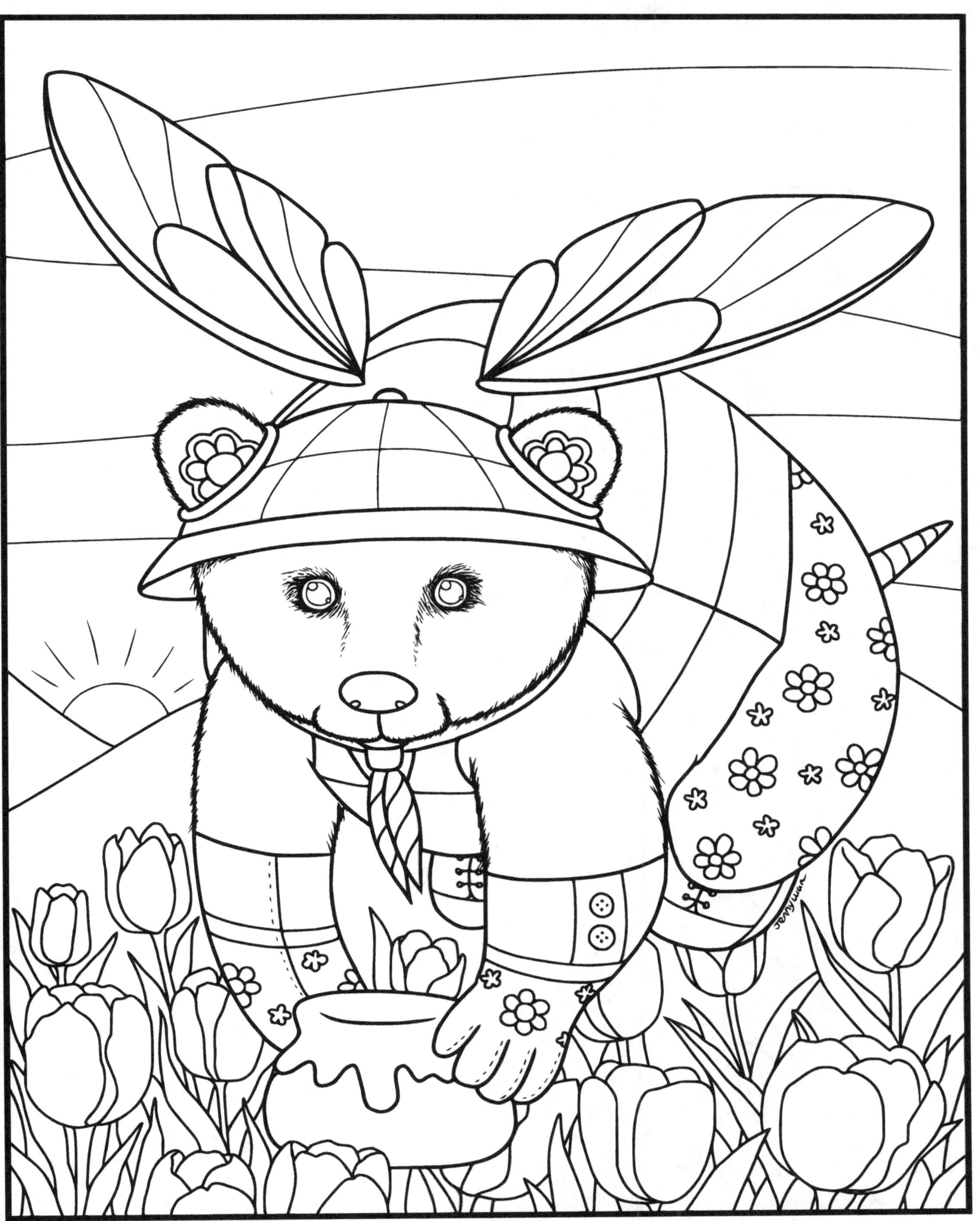

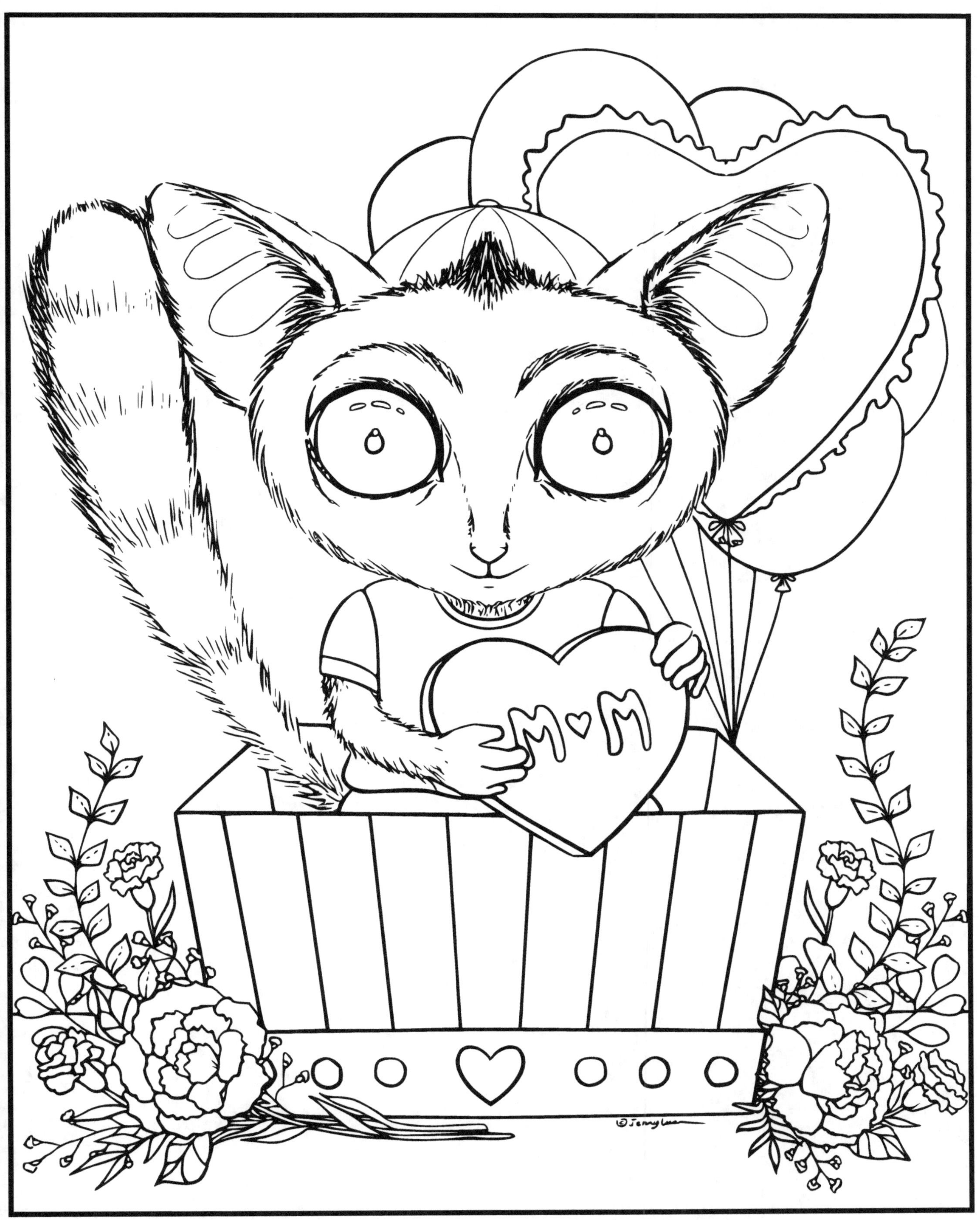
M♥M

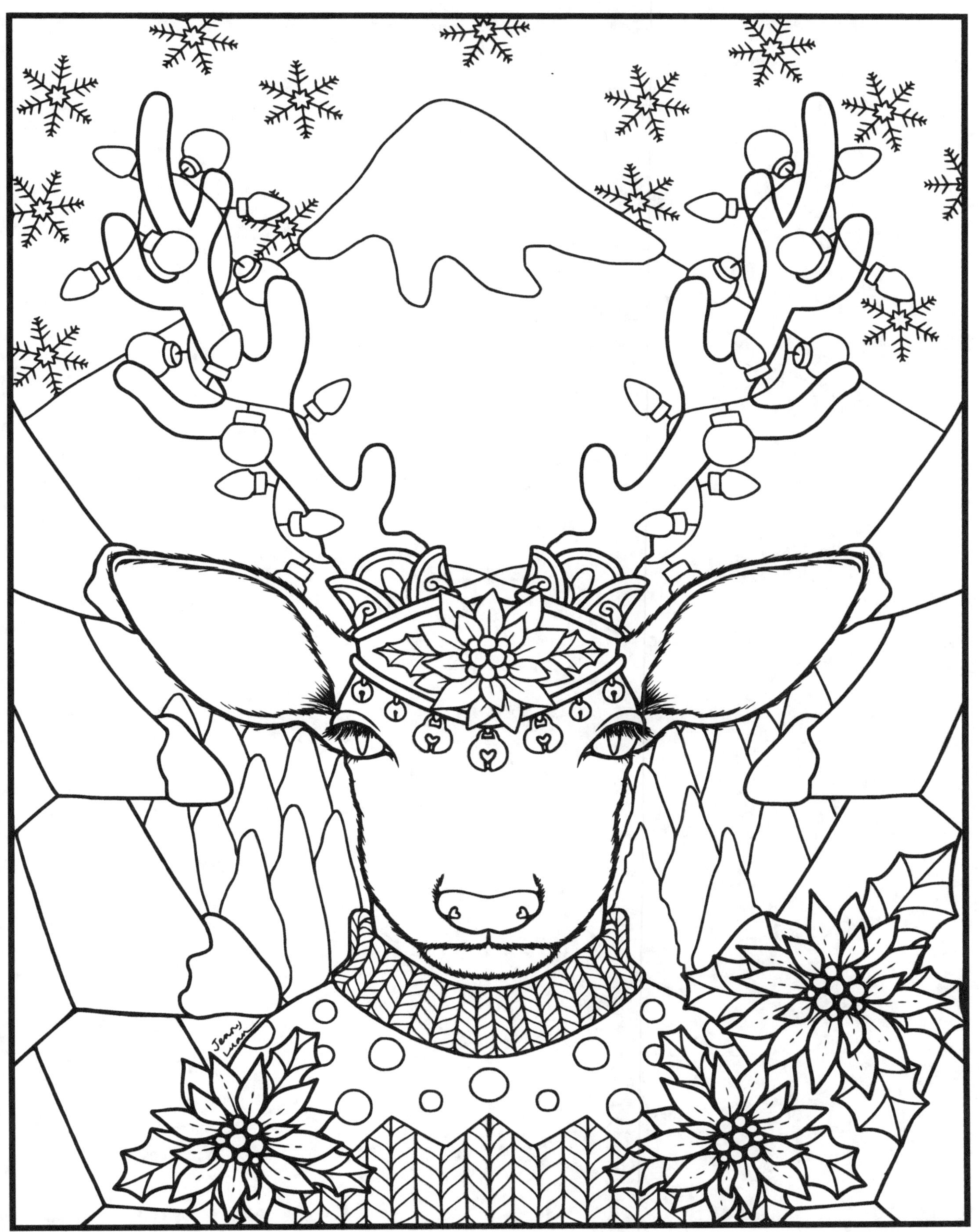

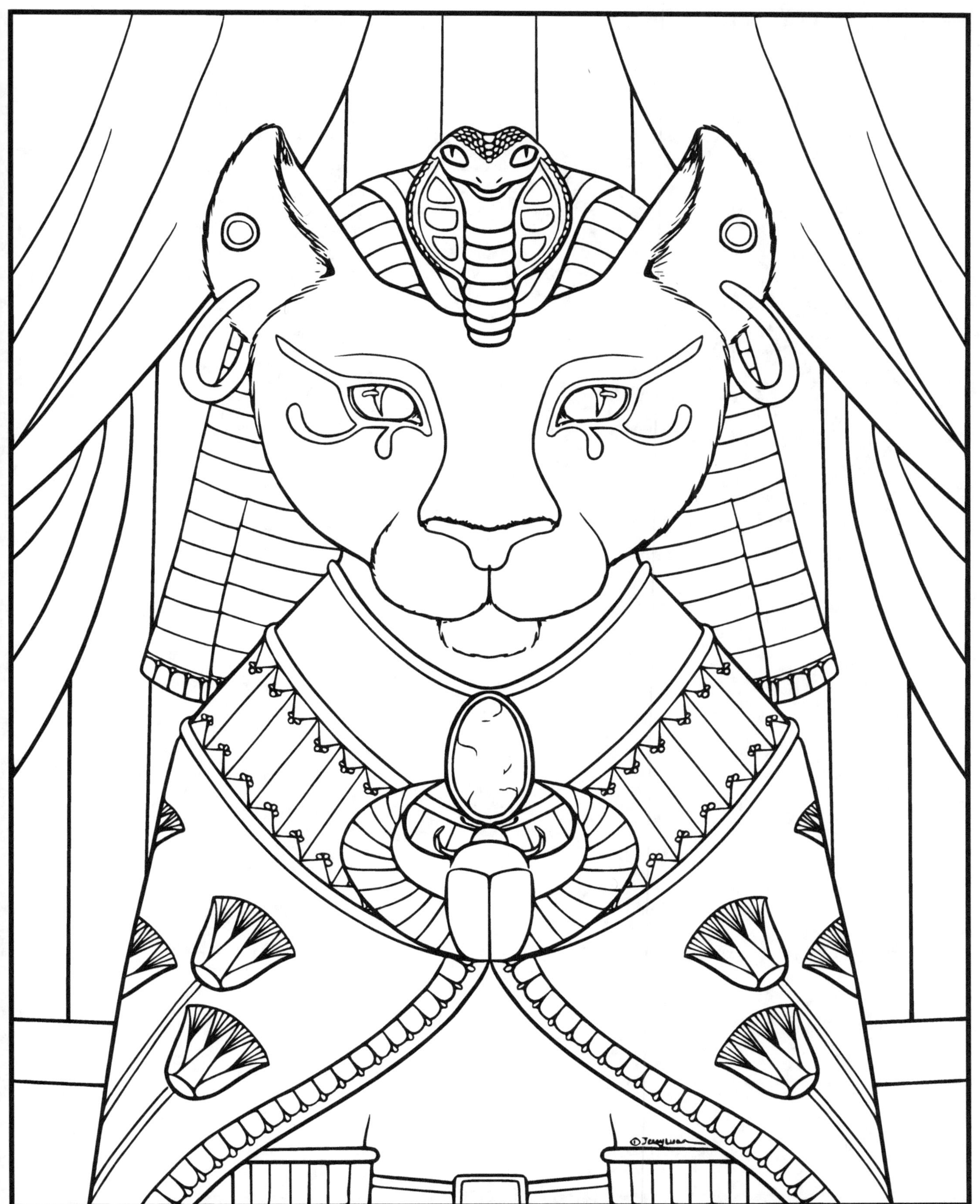

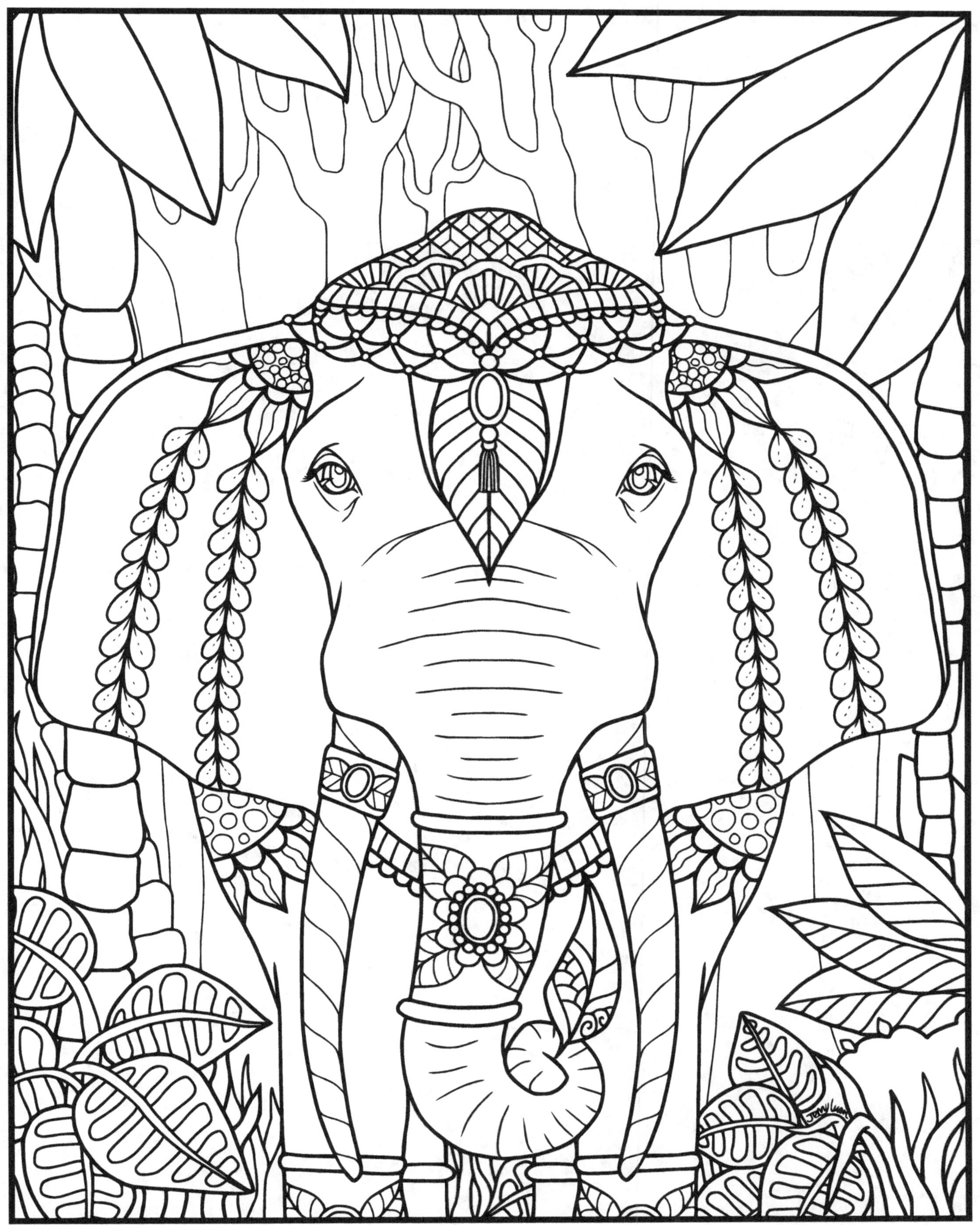

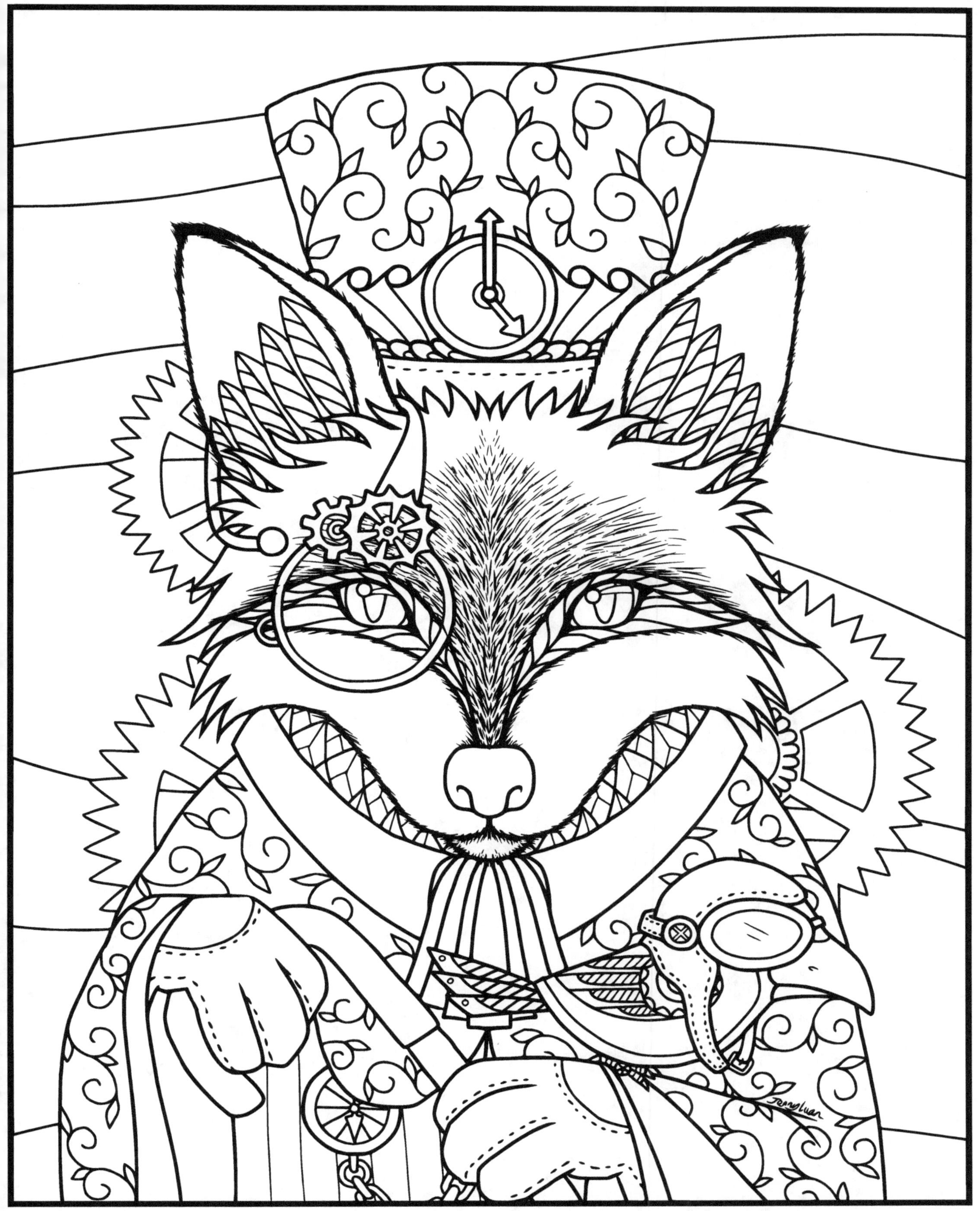

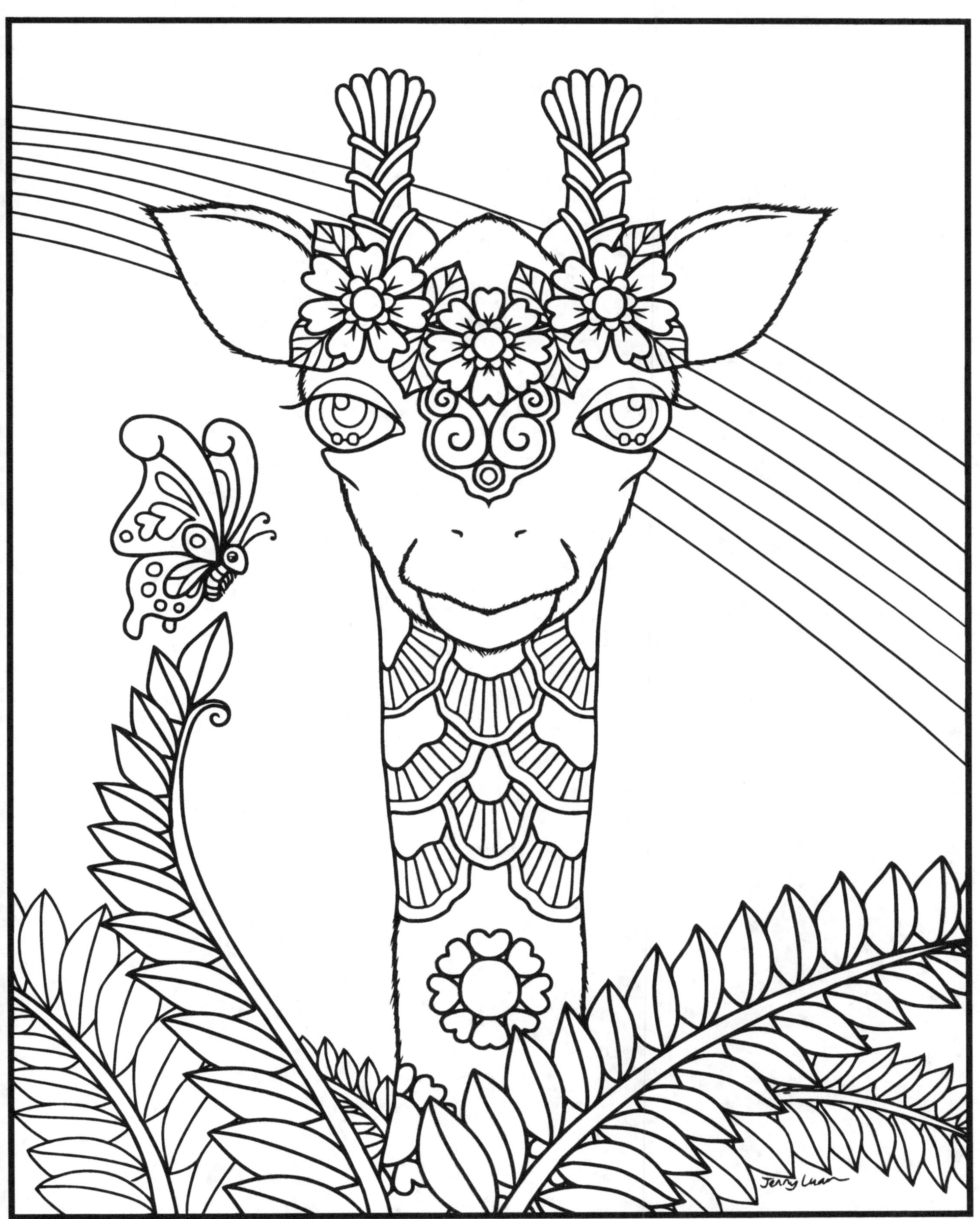

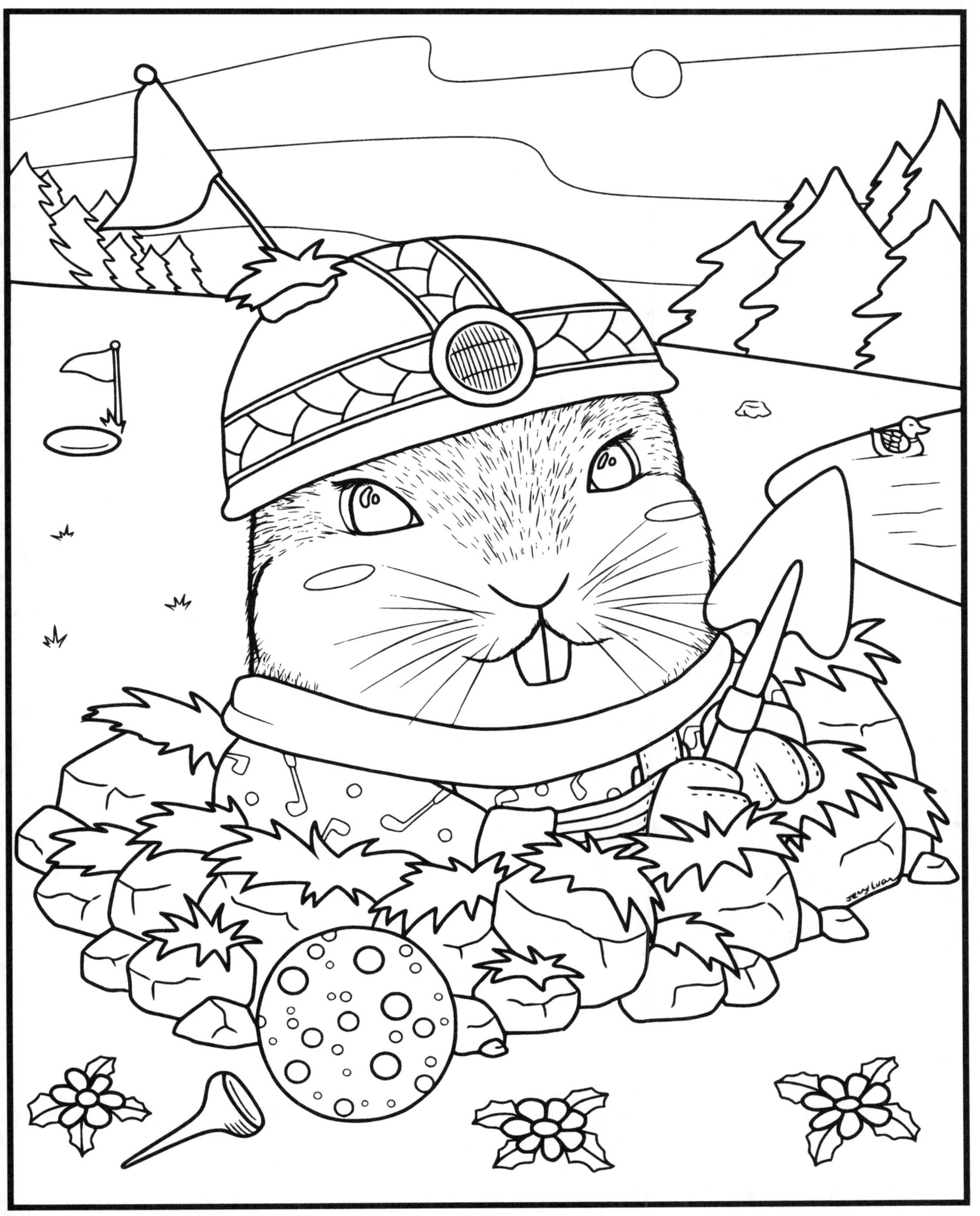

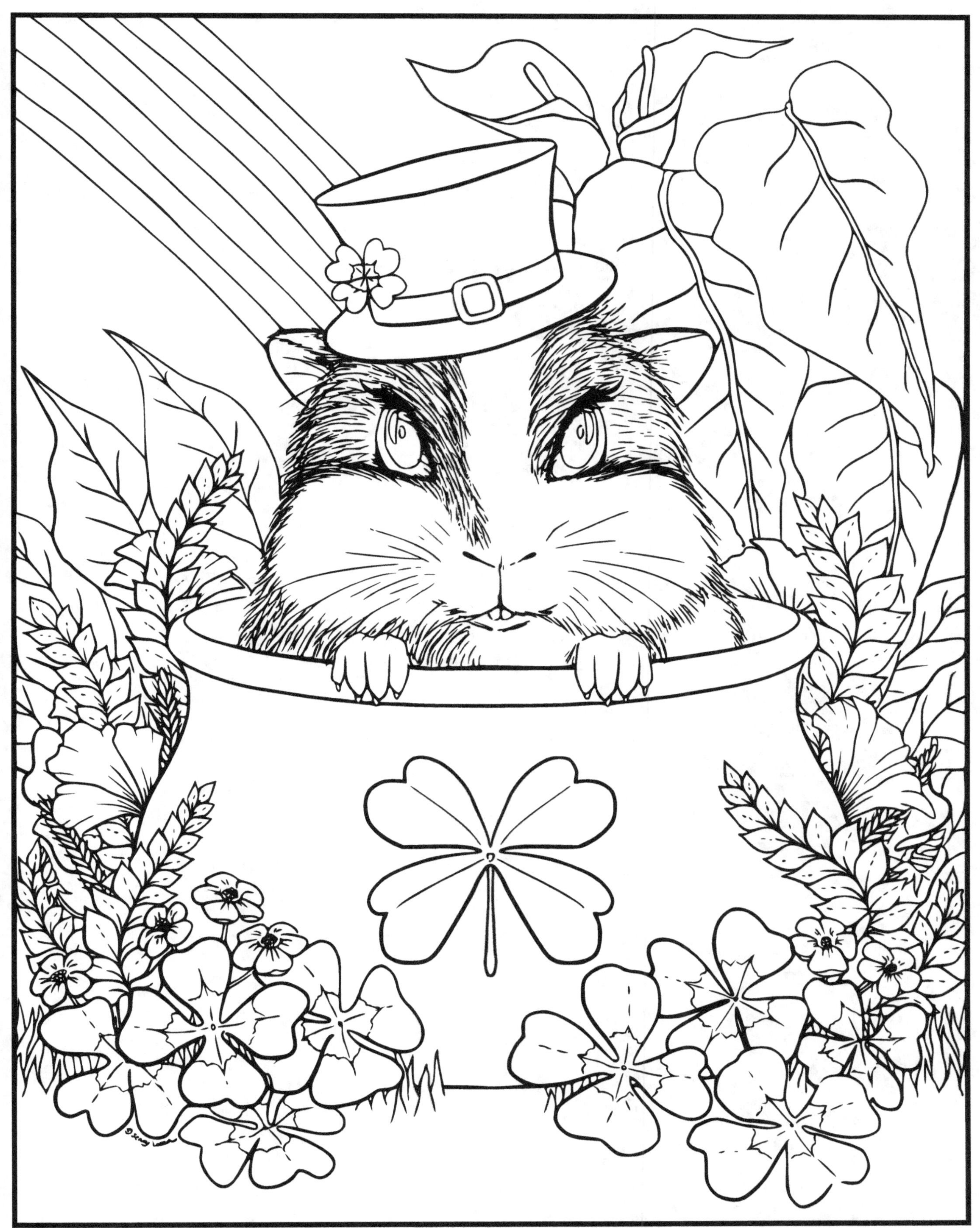

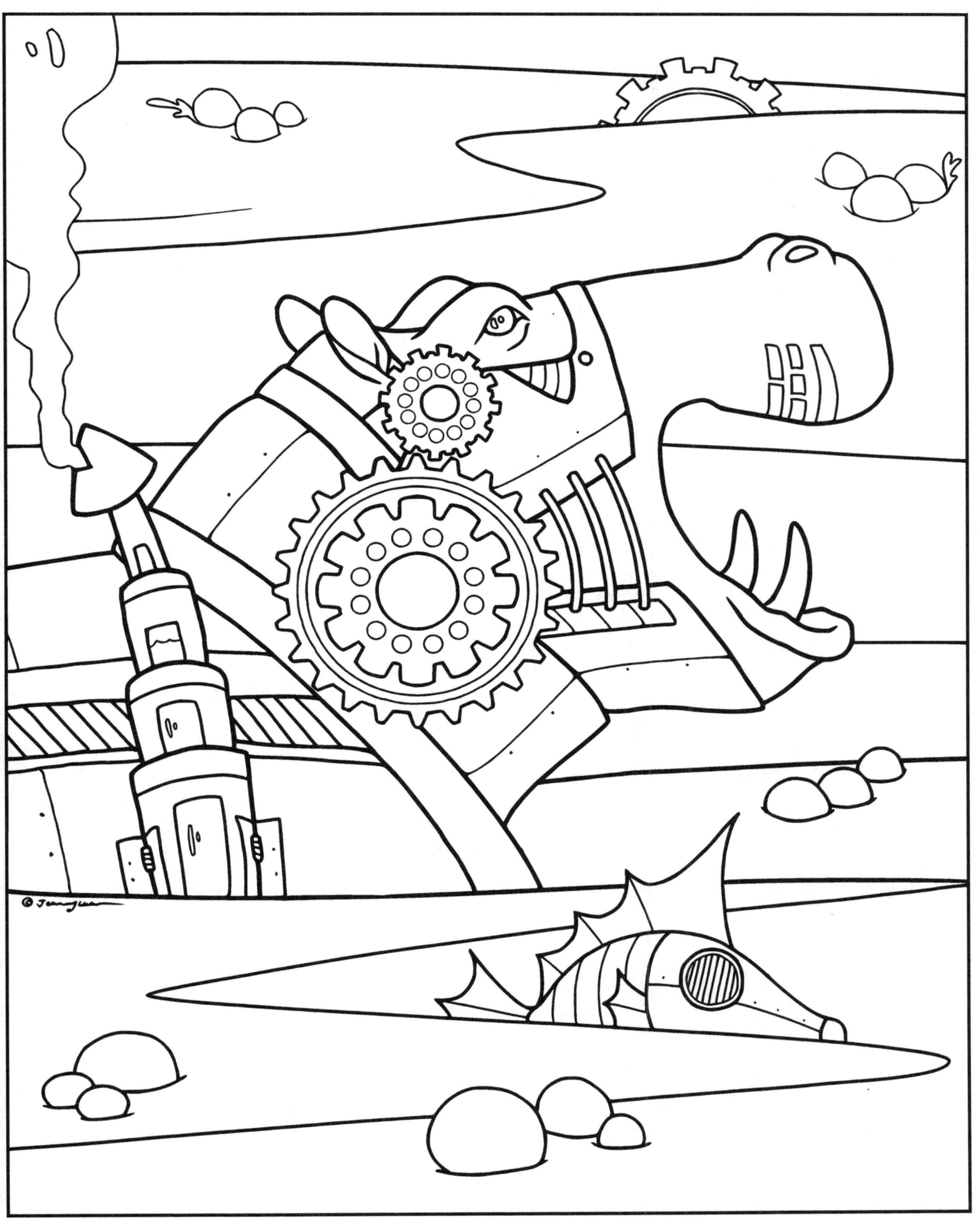

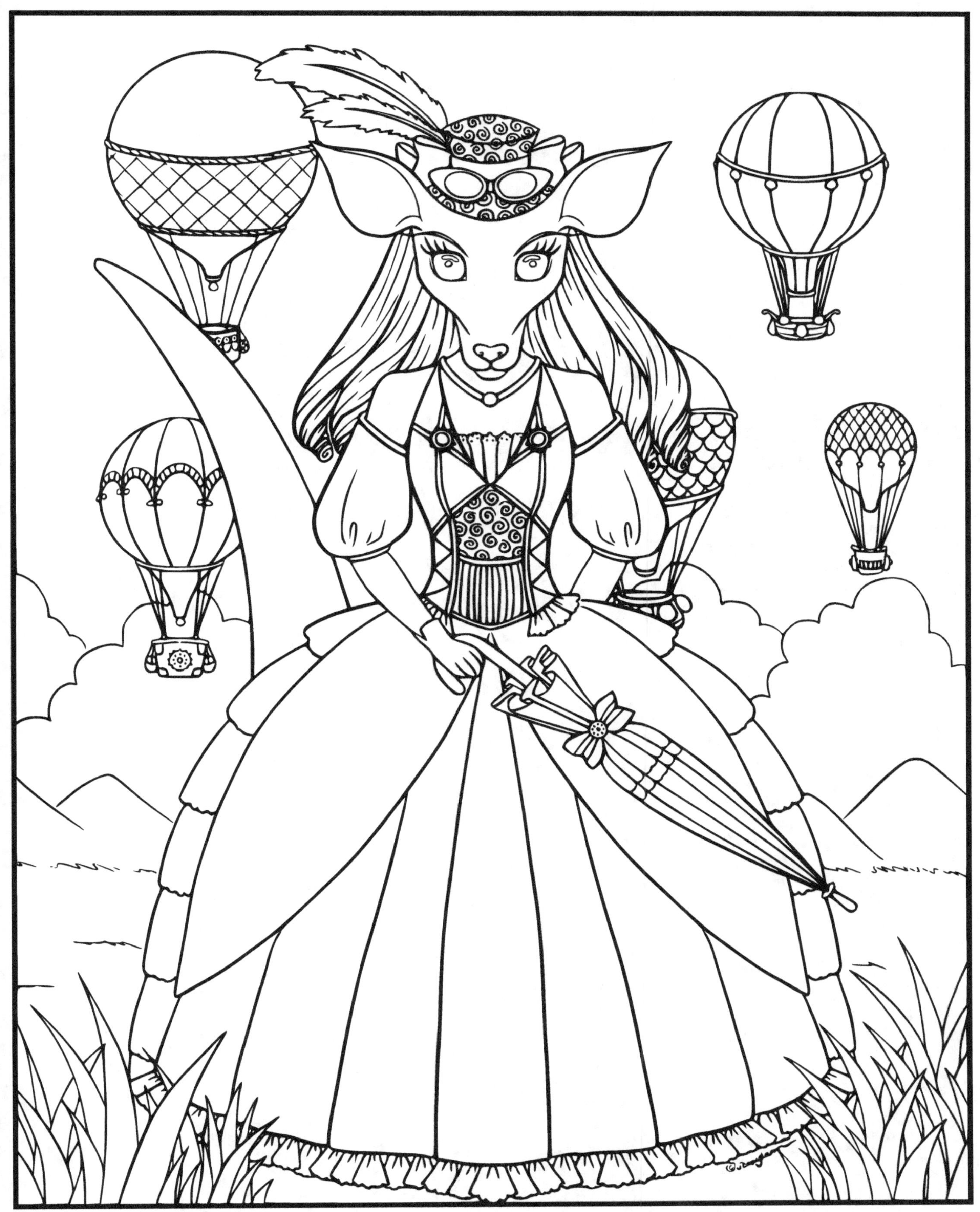

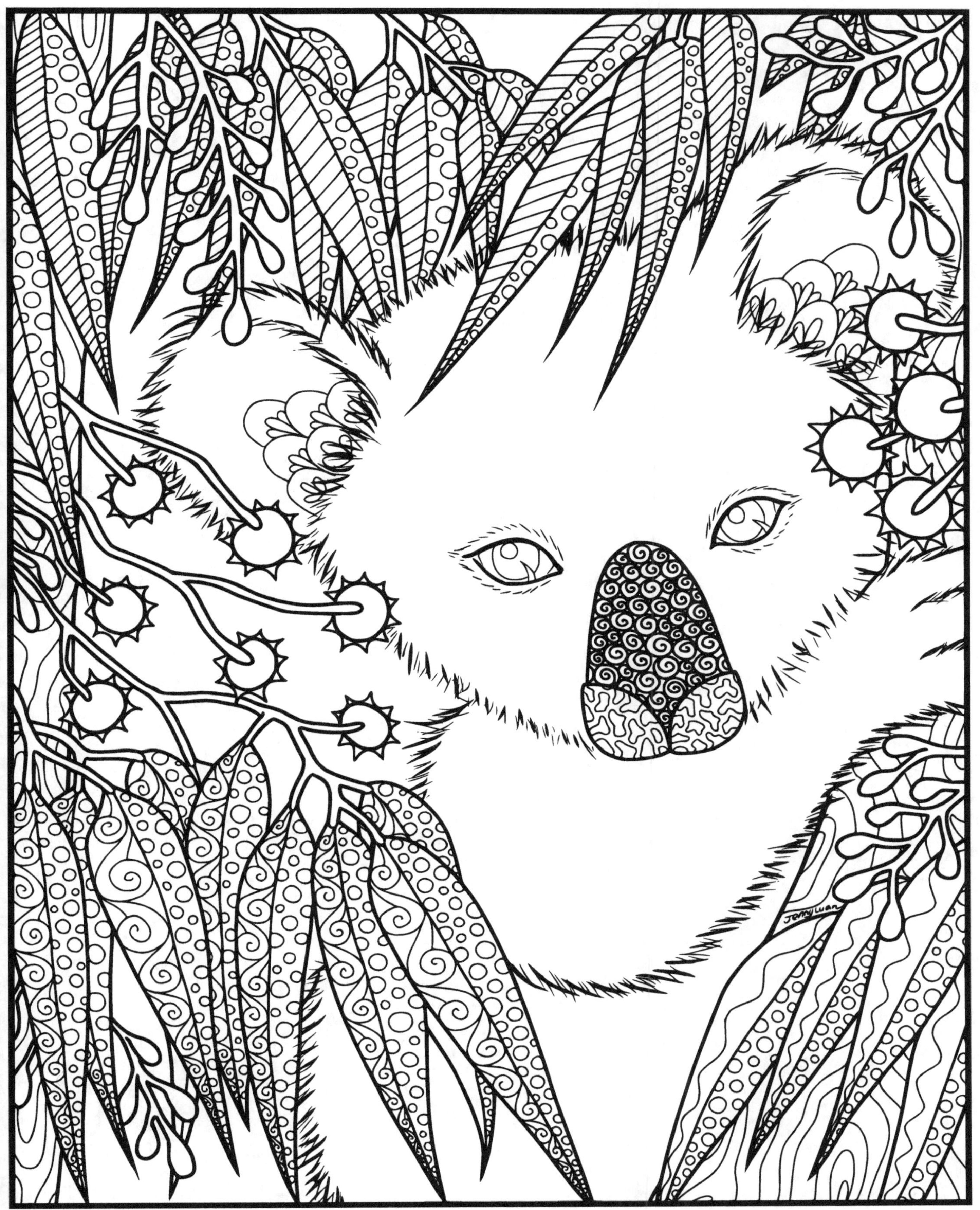

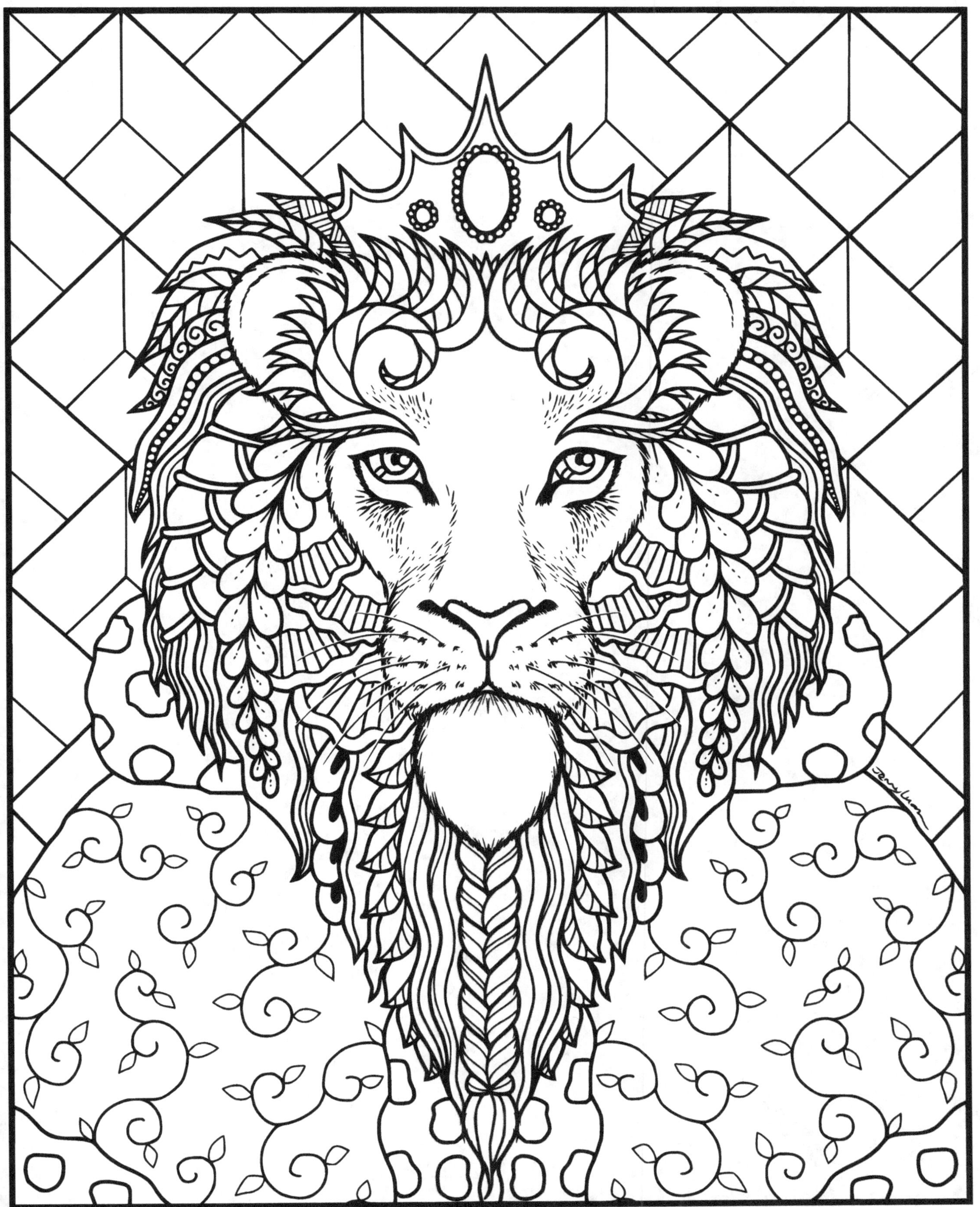

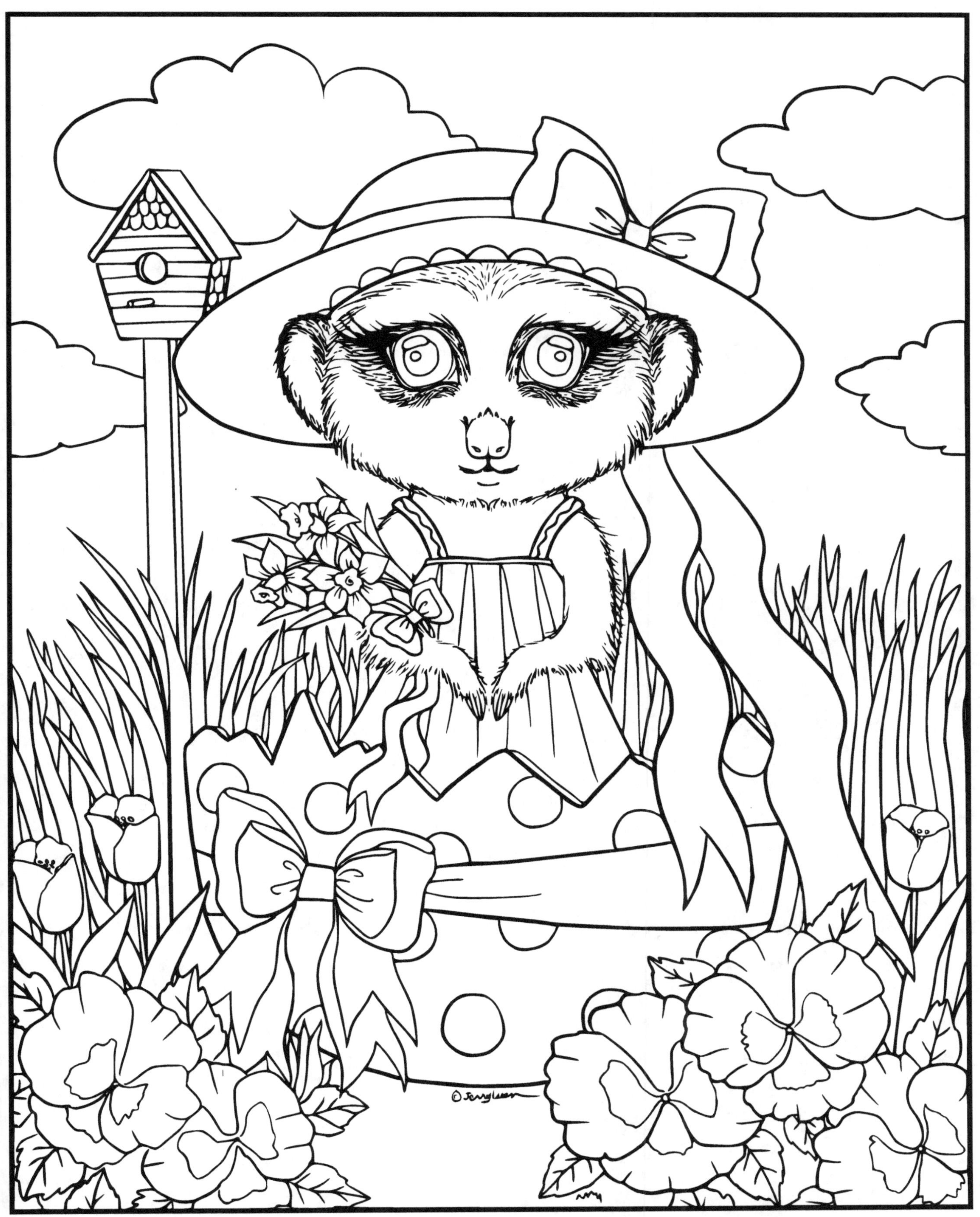

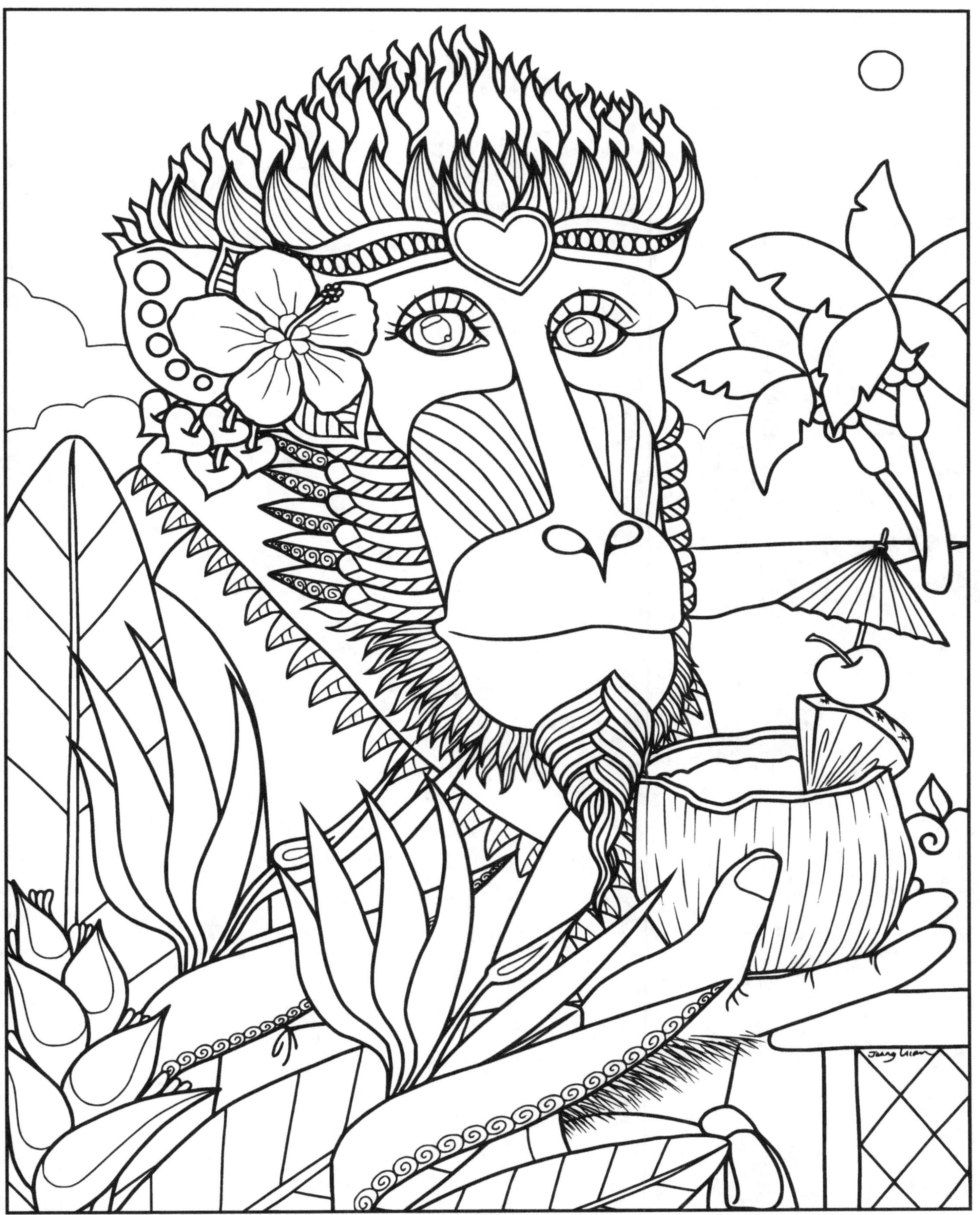

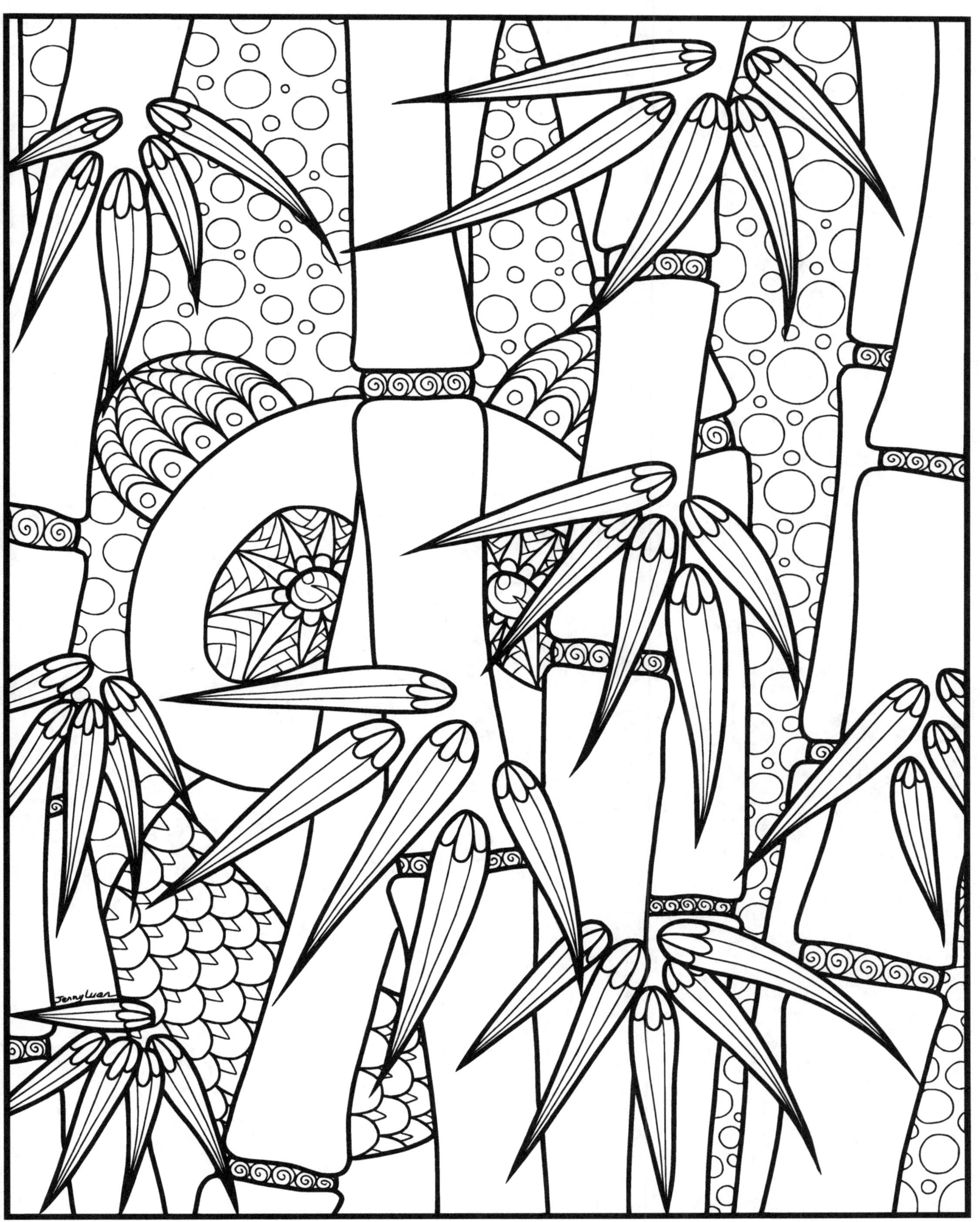

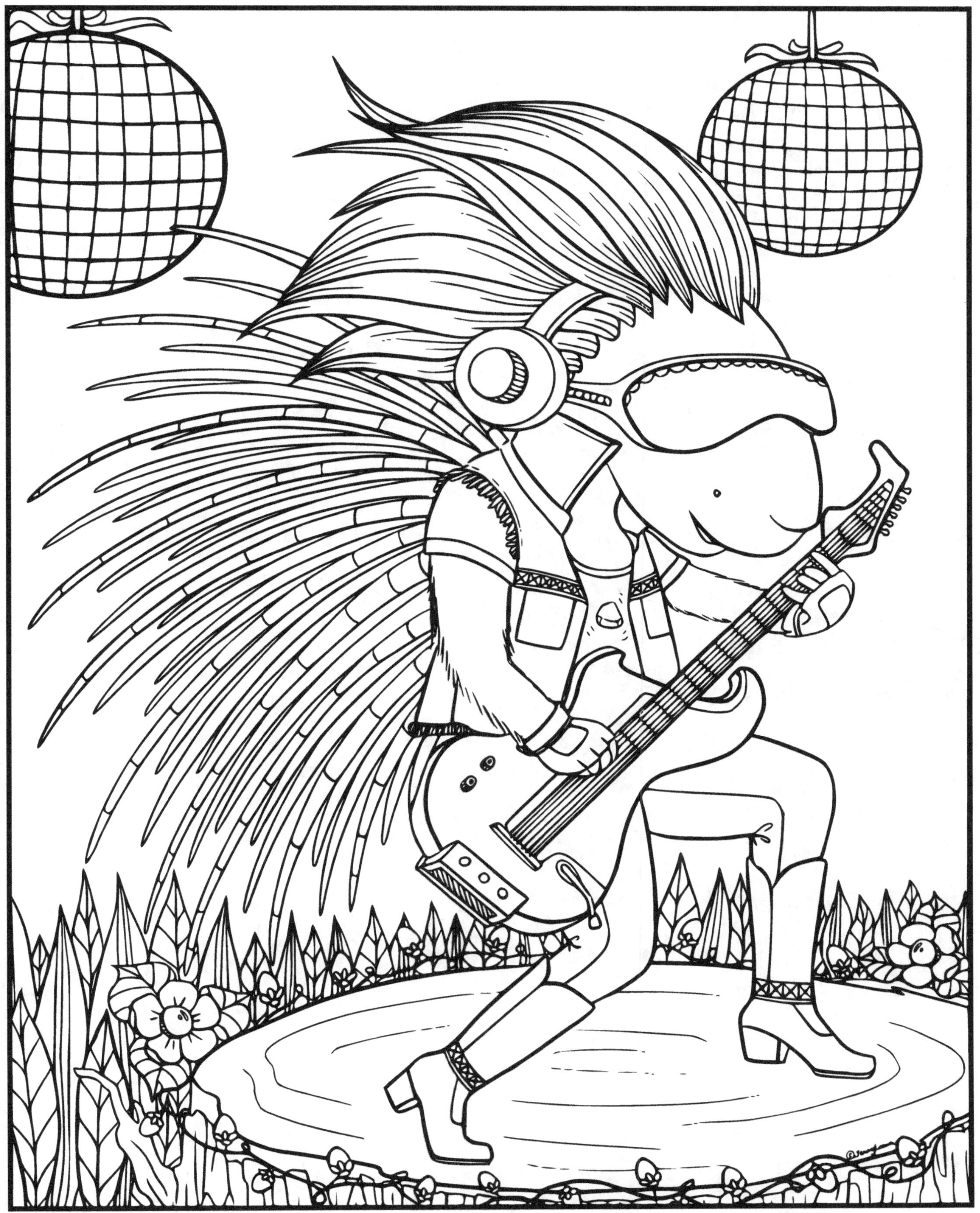

Colored by: ___________________

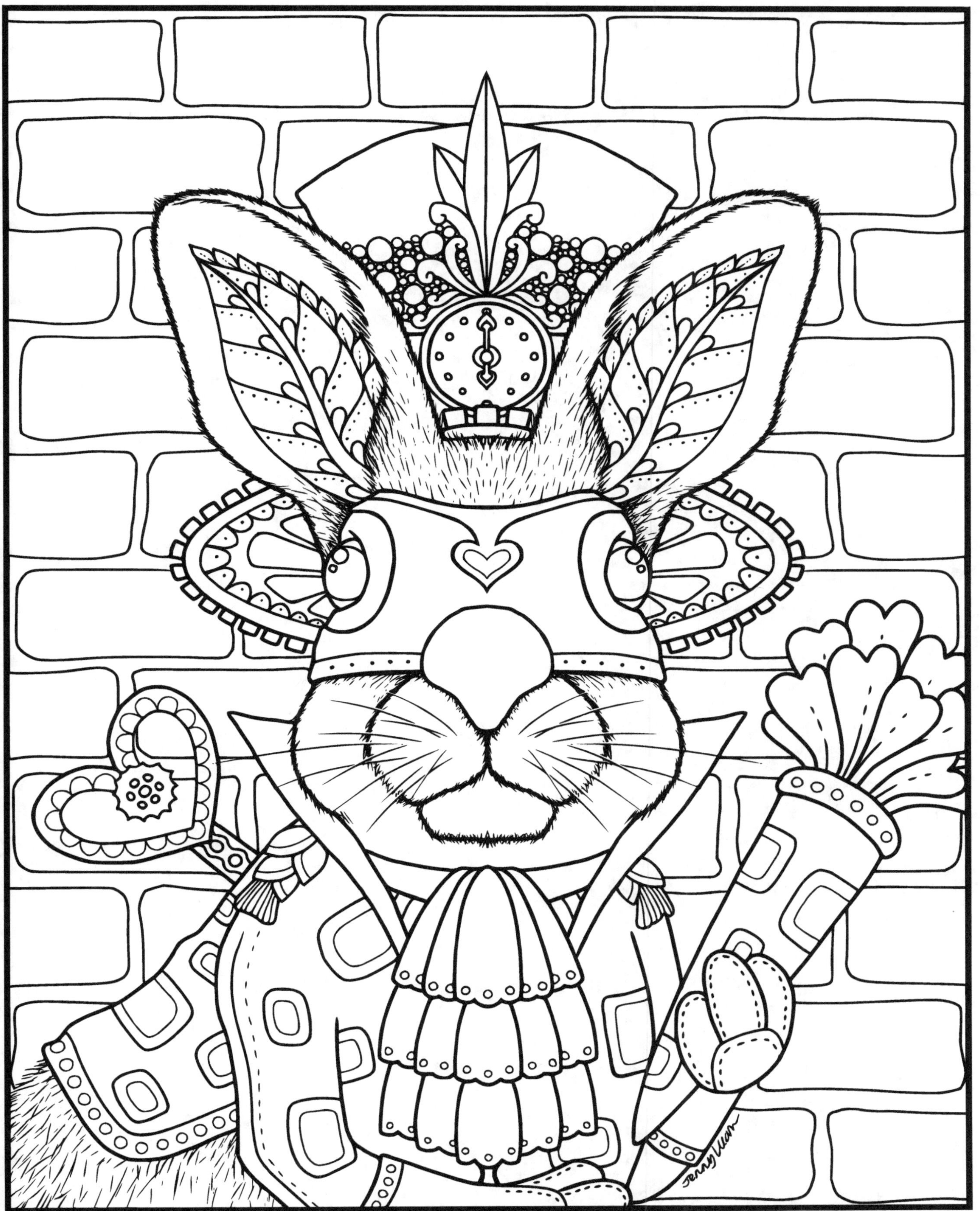

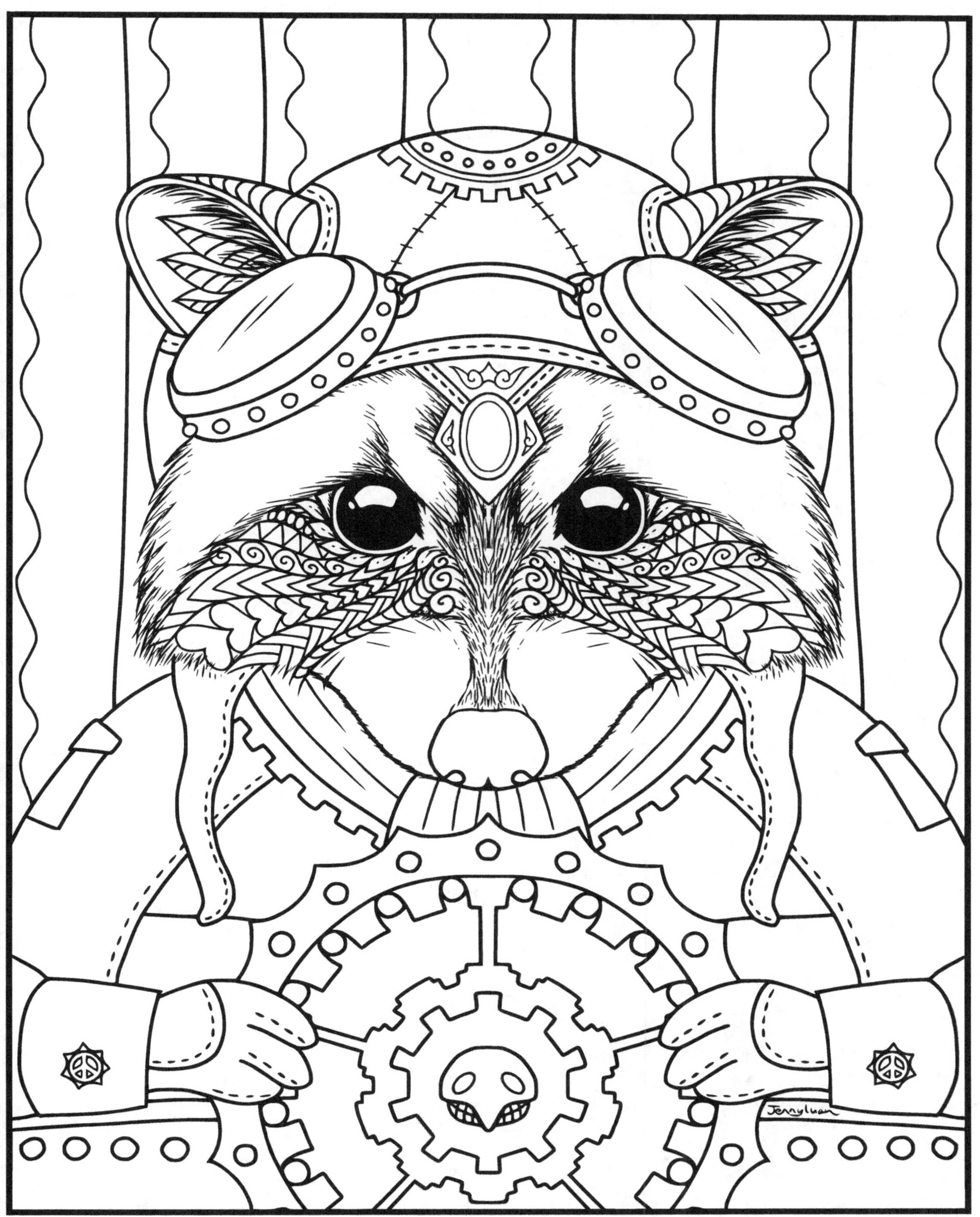

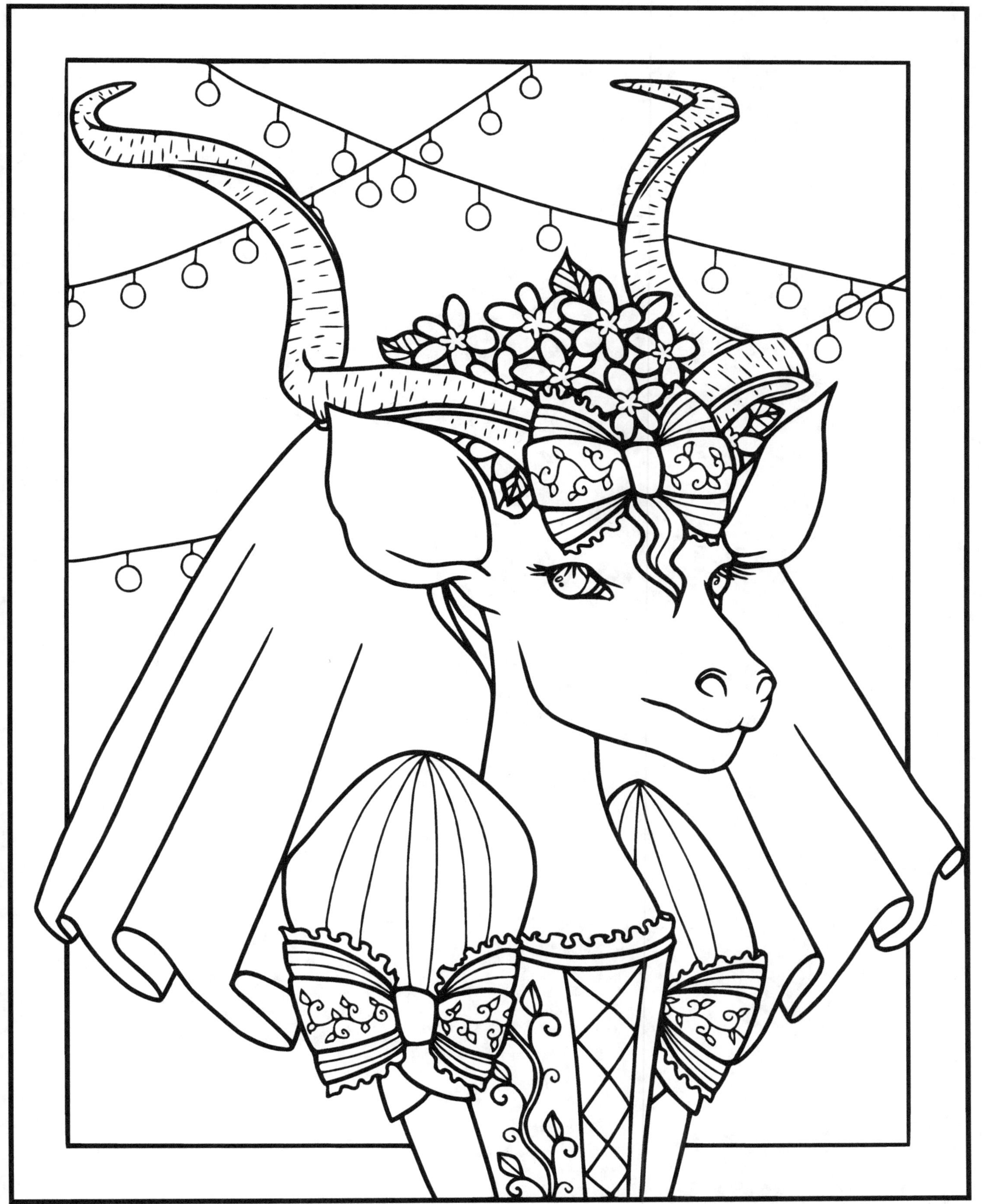

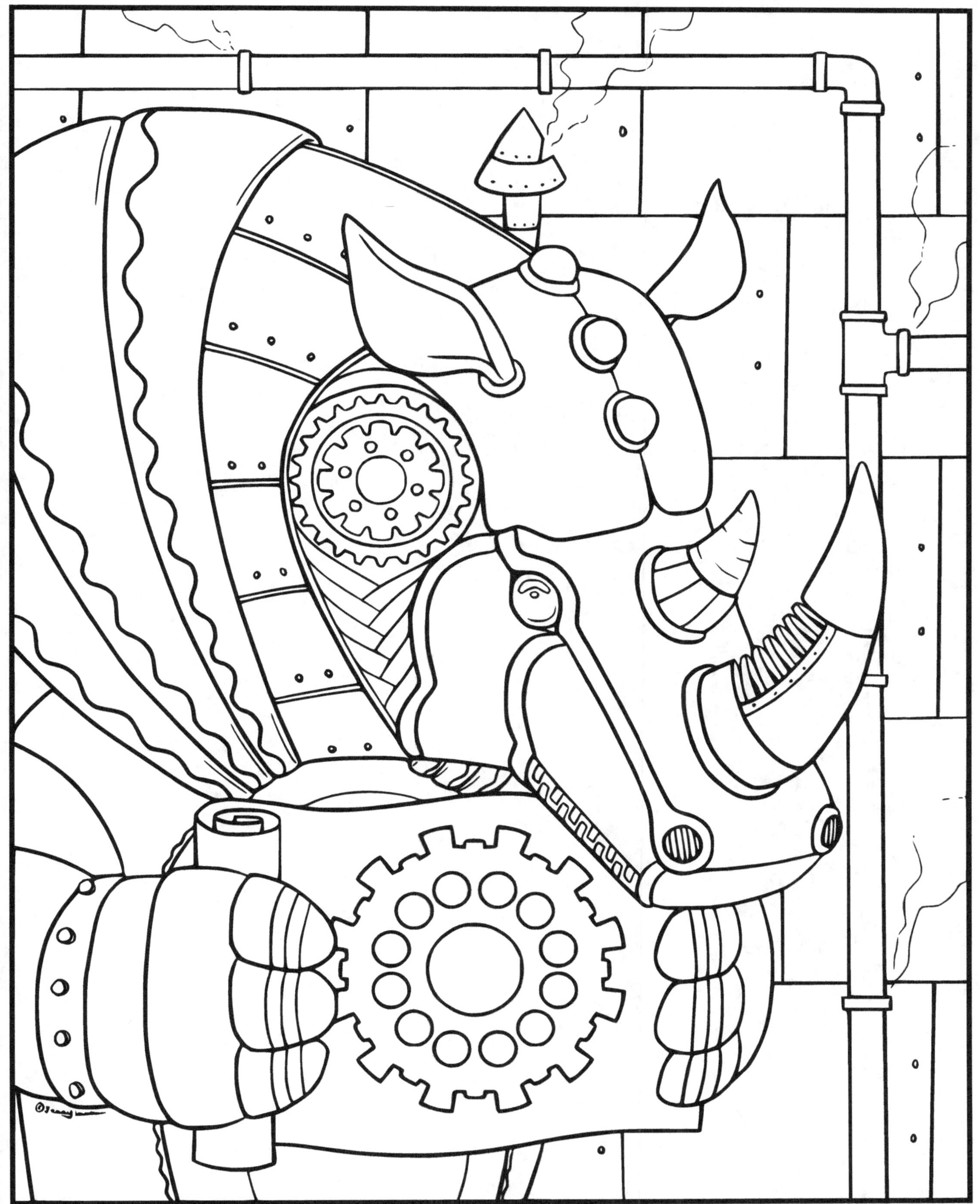

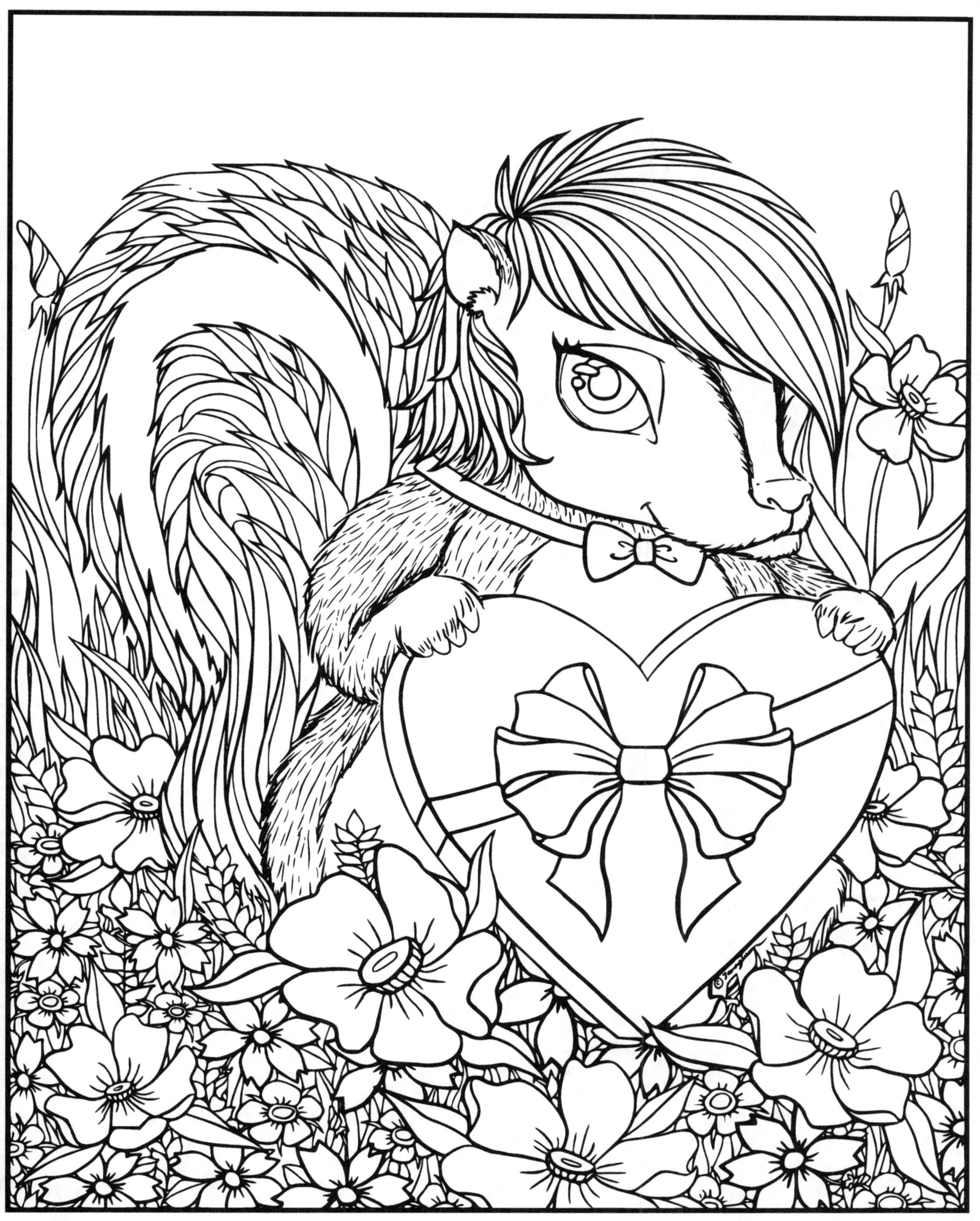

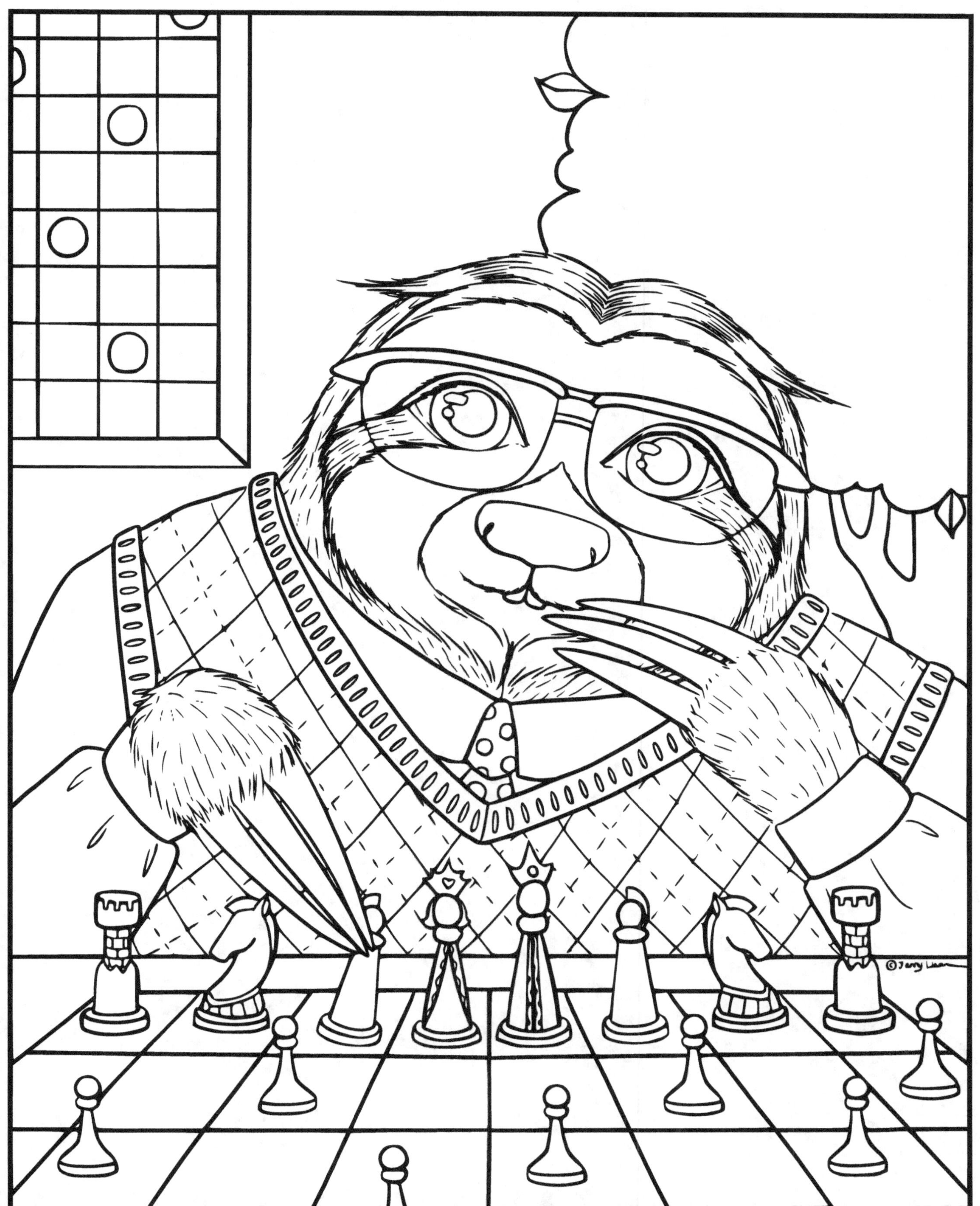

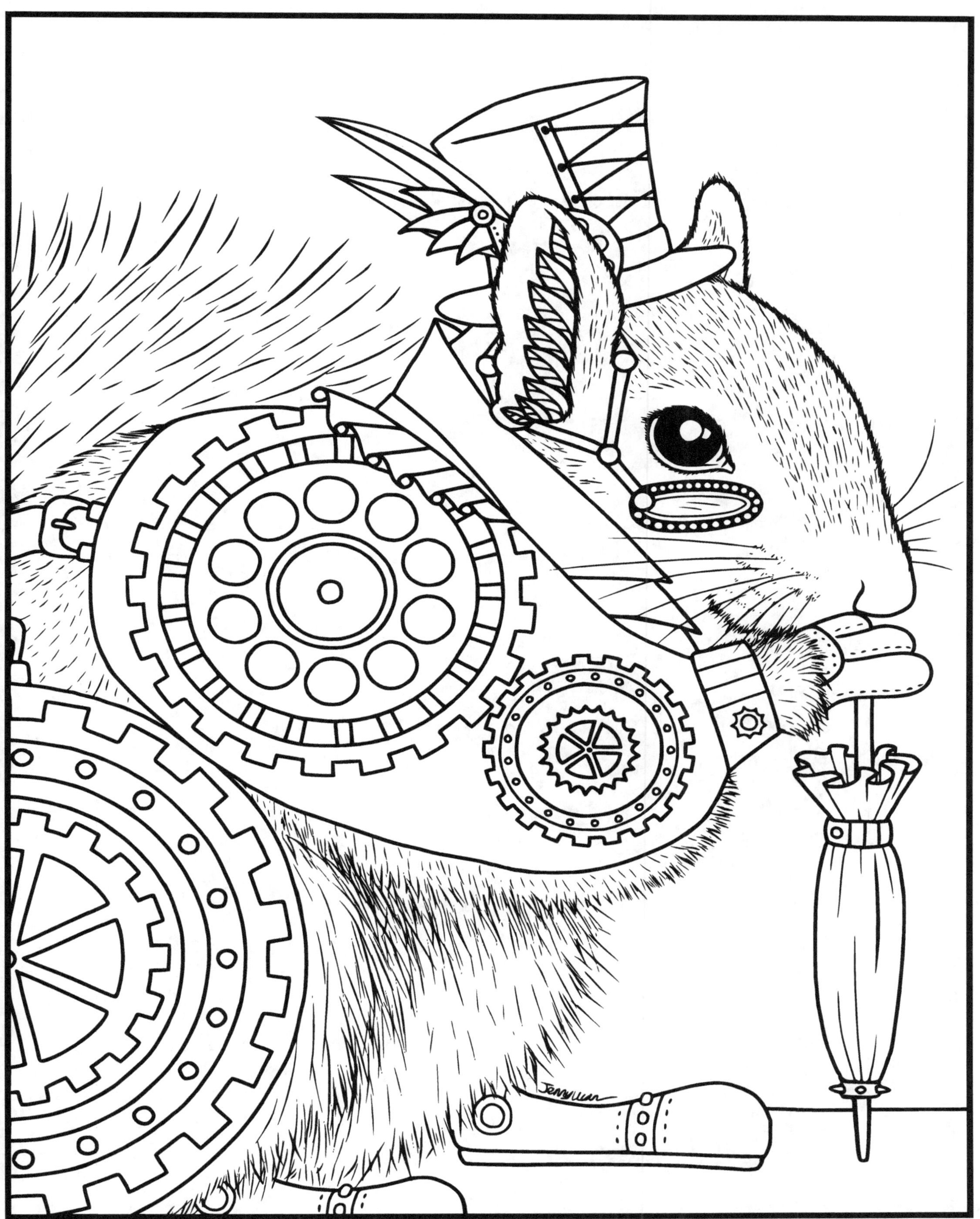

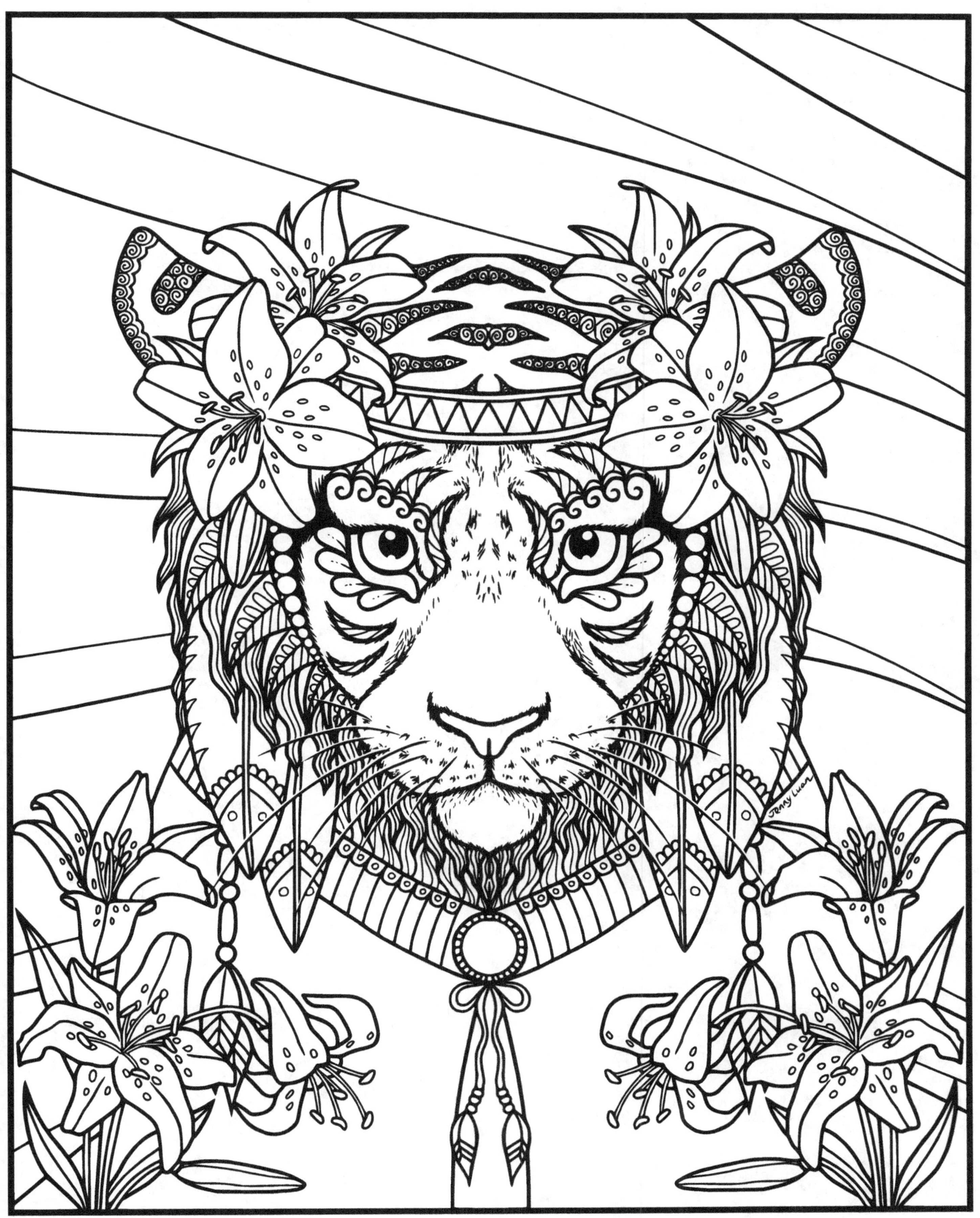

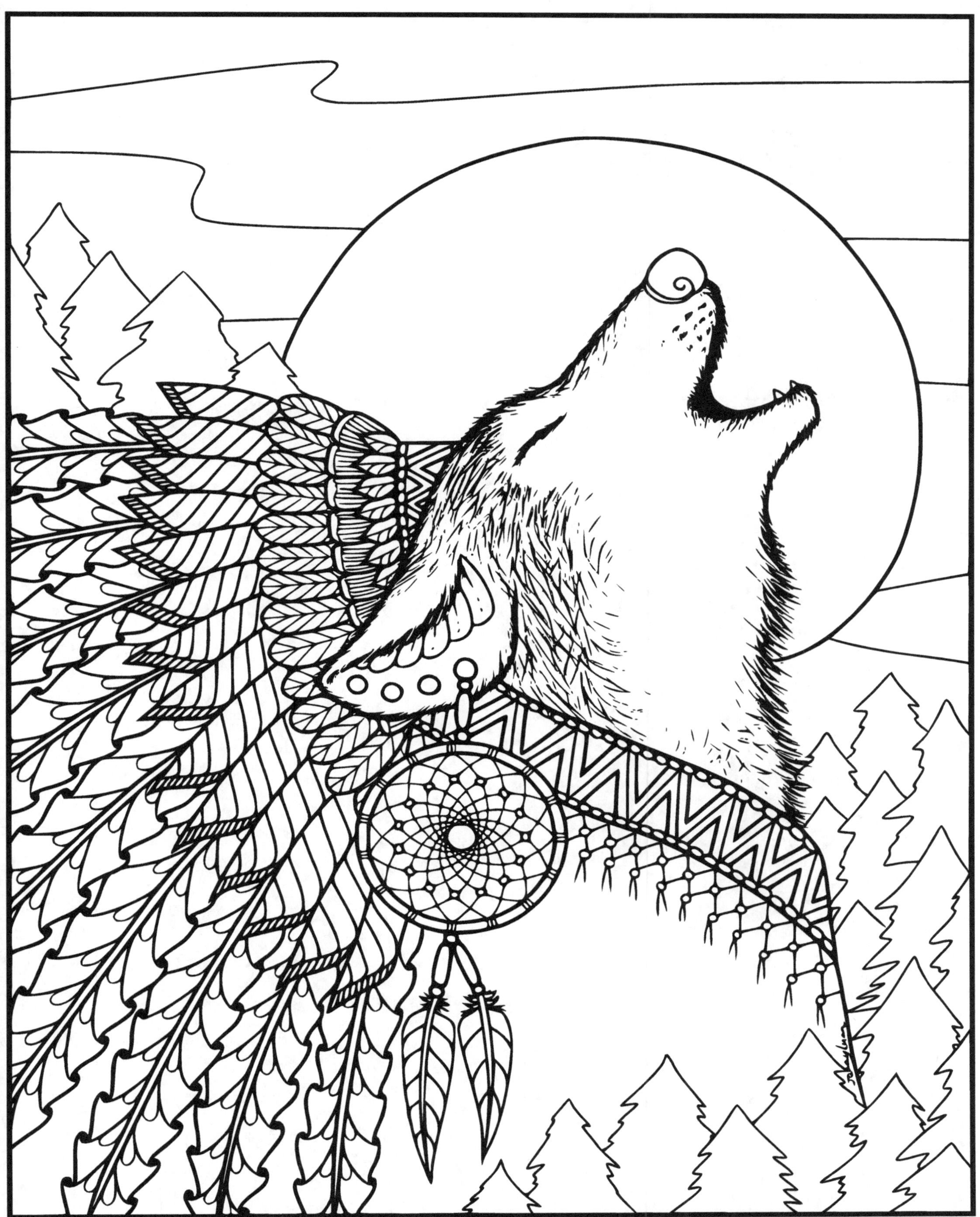

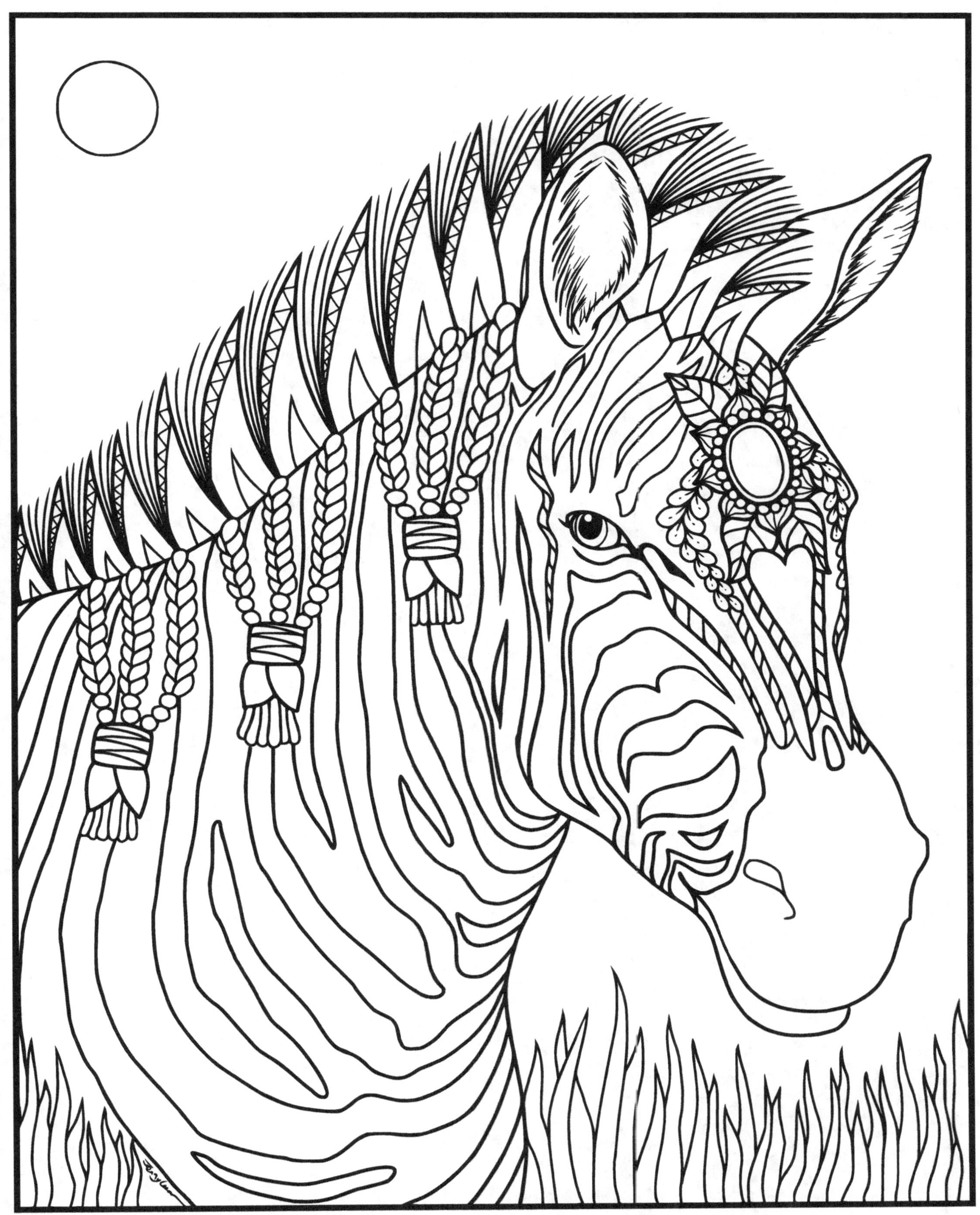

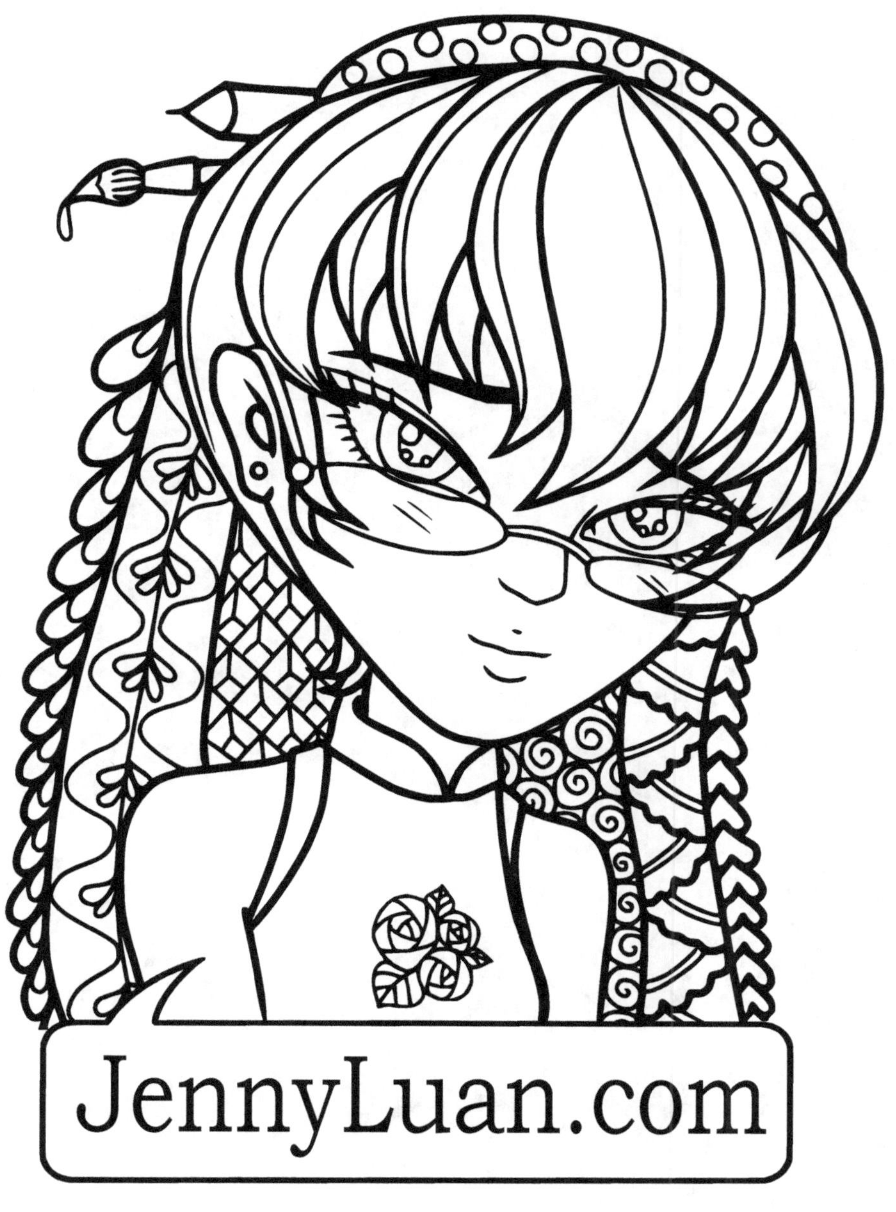

Please
check out
my
other books

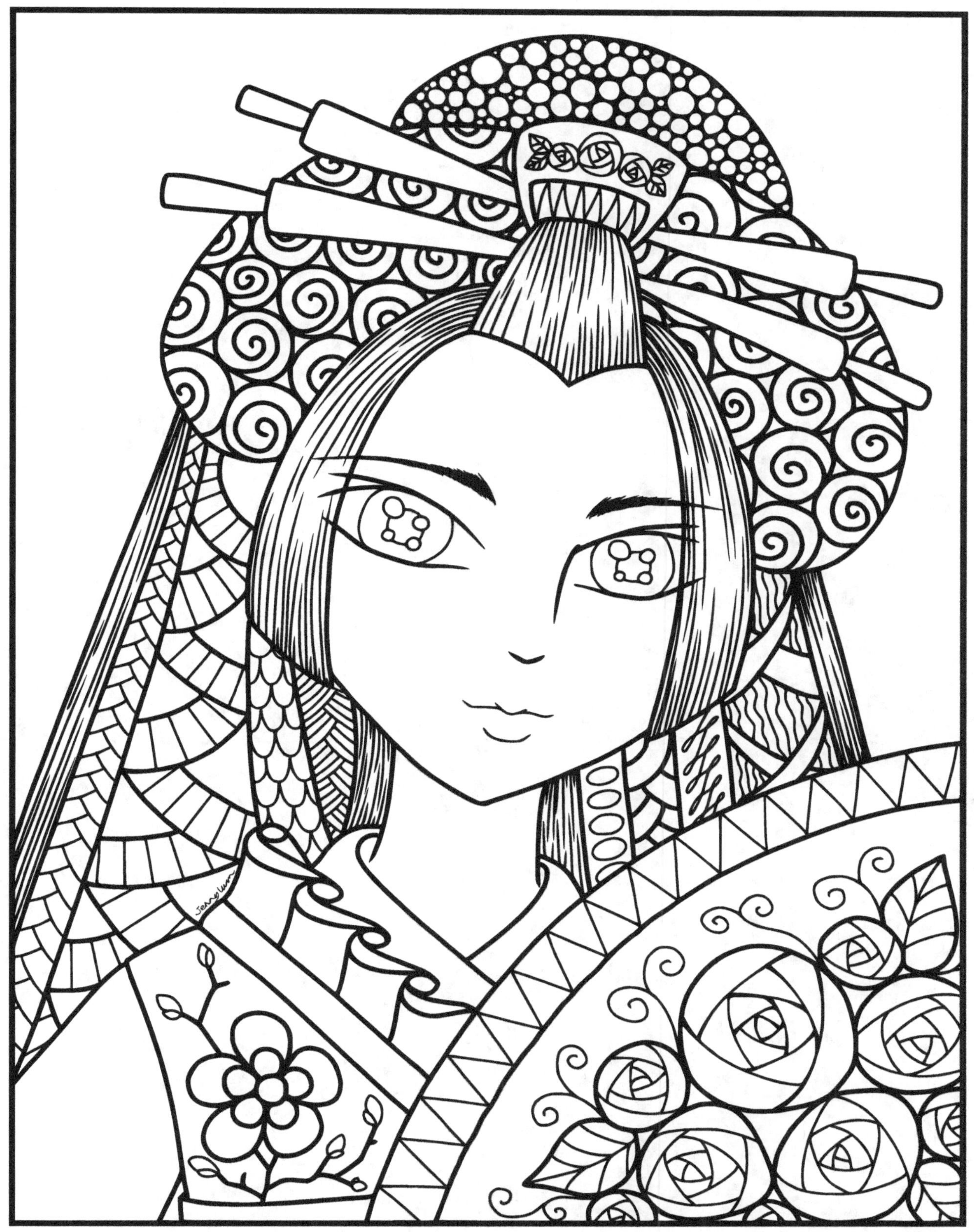

Colorist: ___________________________

Anime Doodle Girls by JennyLuanArt

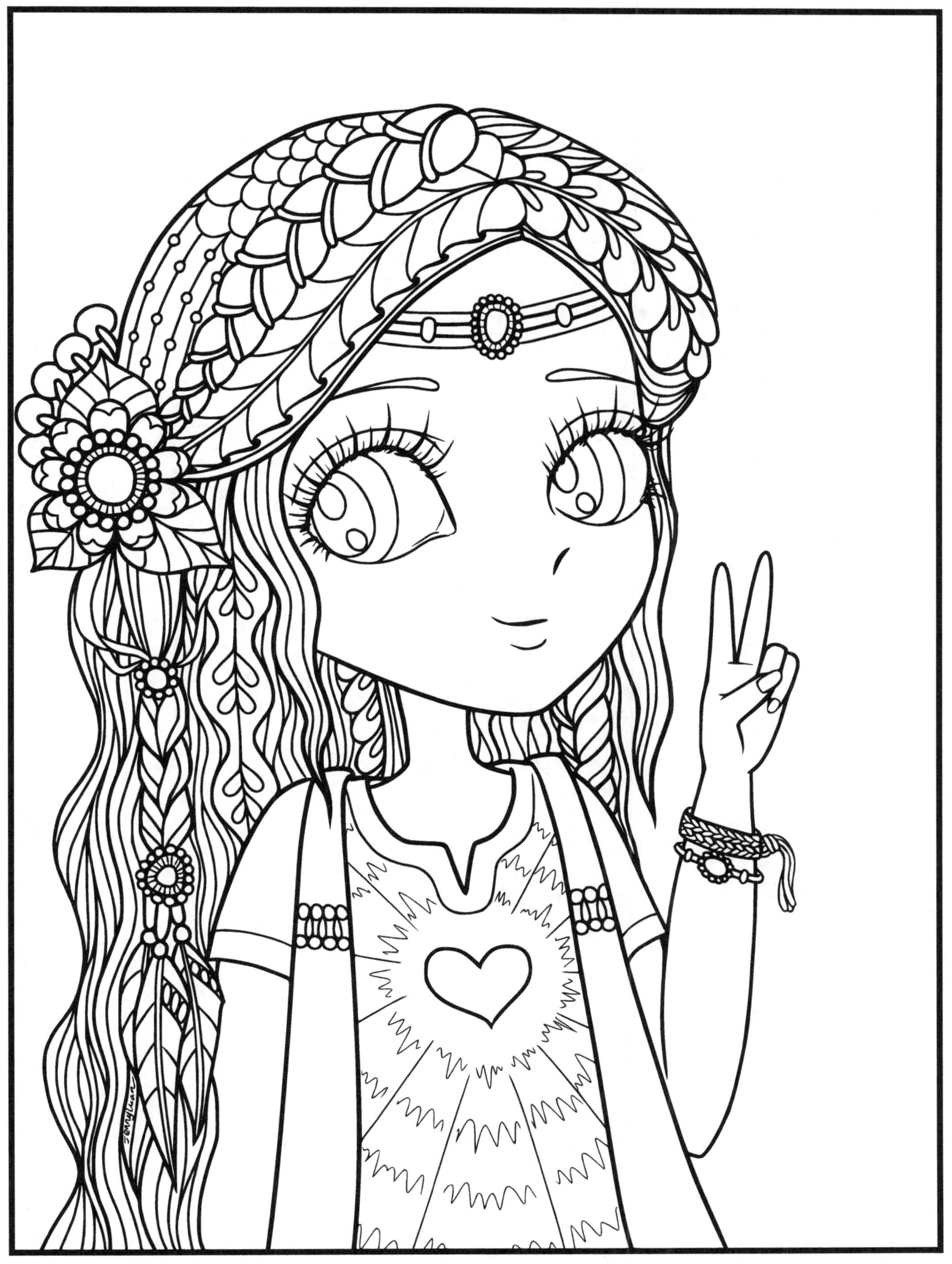

Colored by _______________

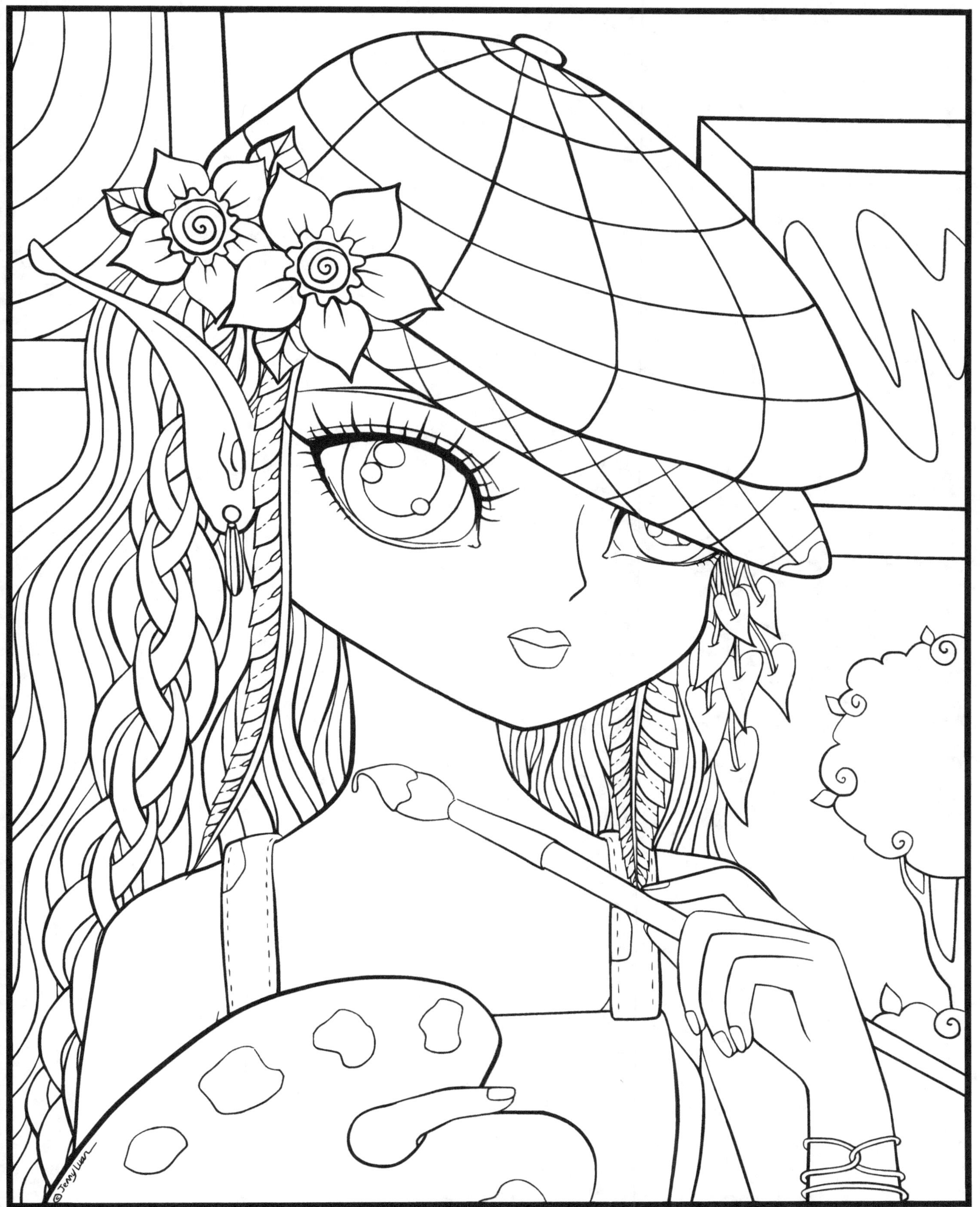

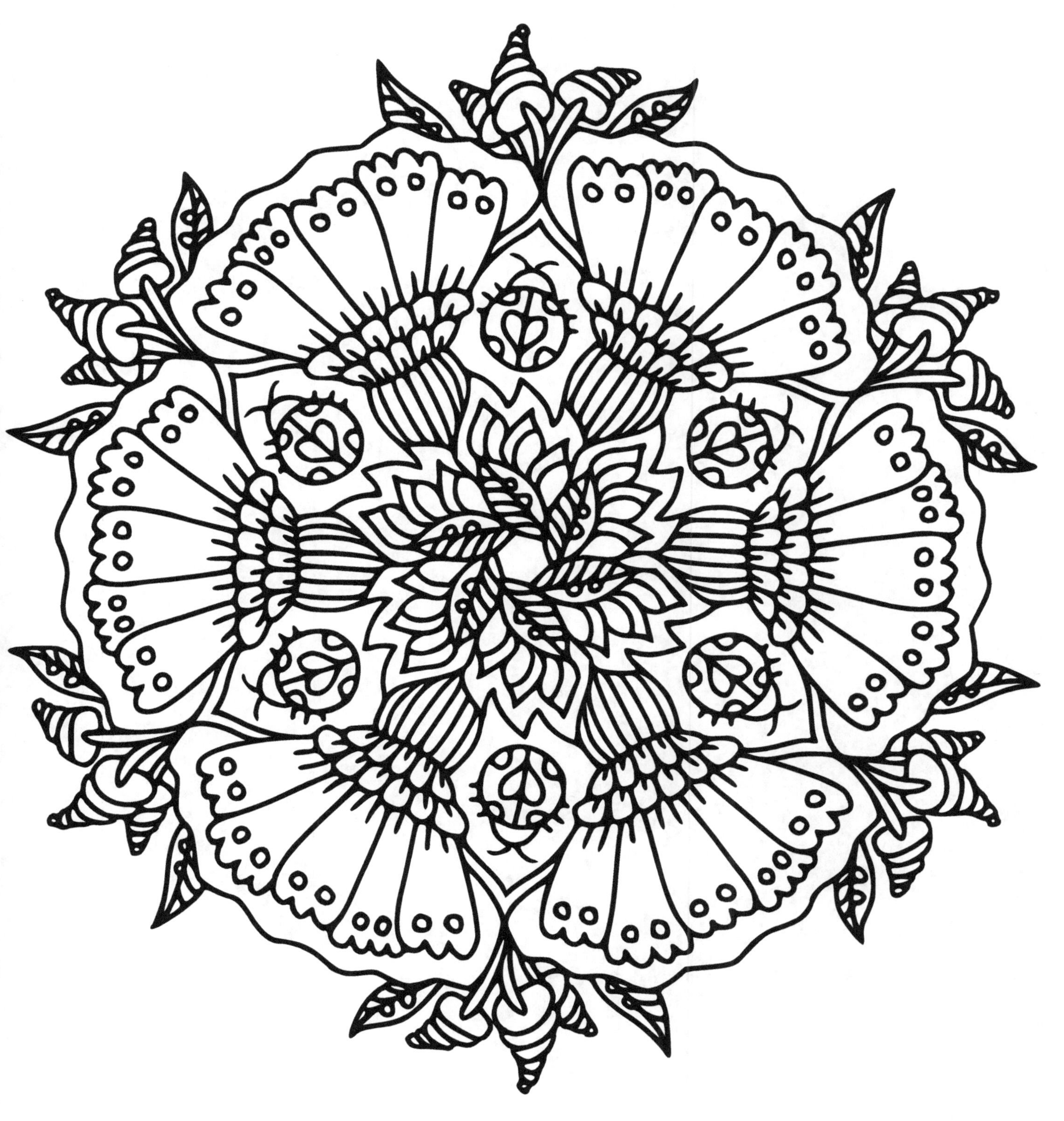

Mandala Doodle Flowers by JennyLuanArt

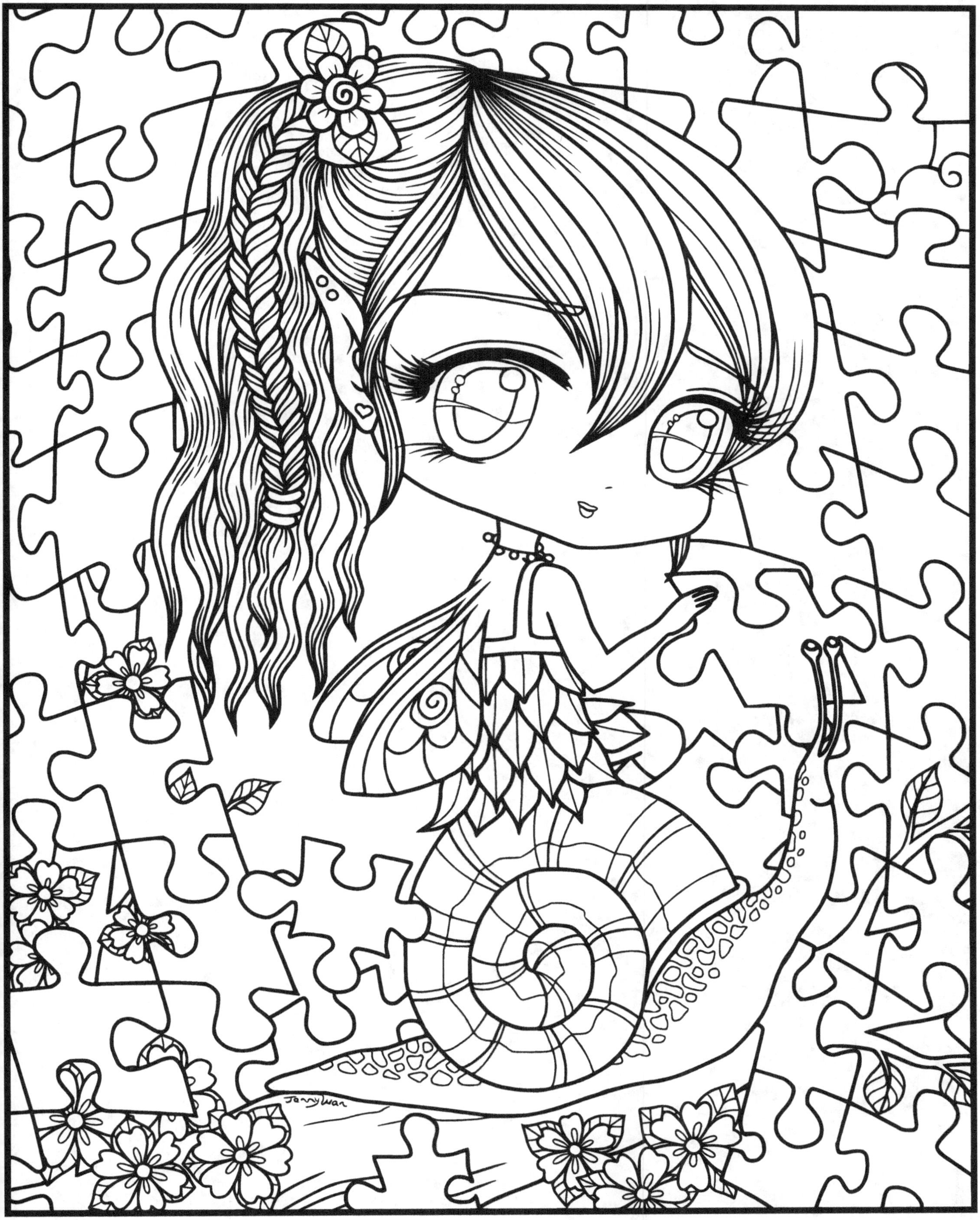

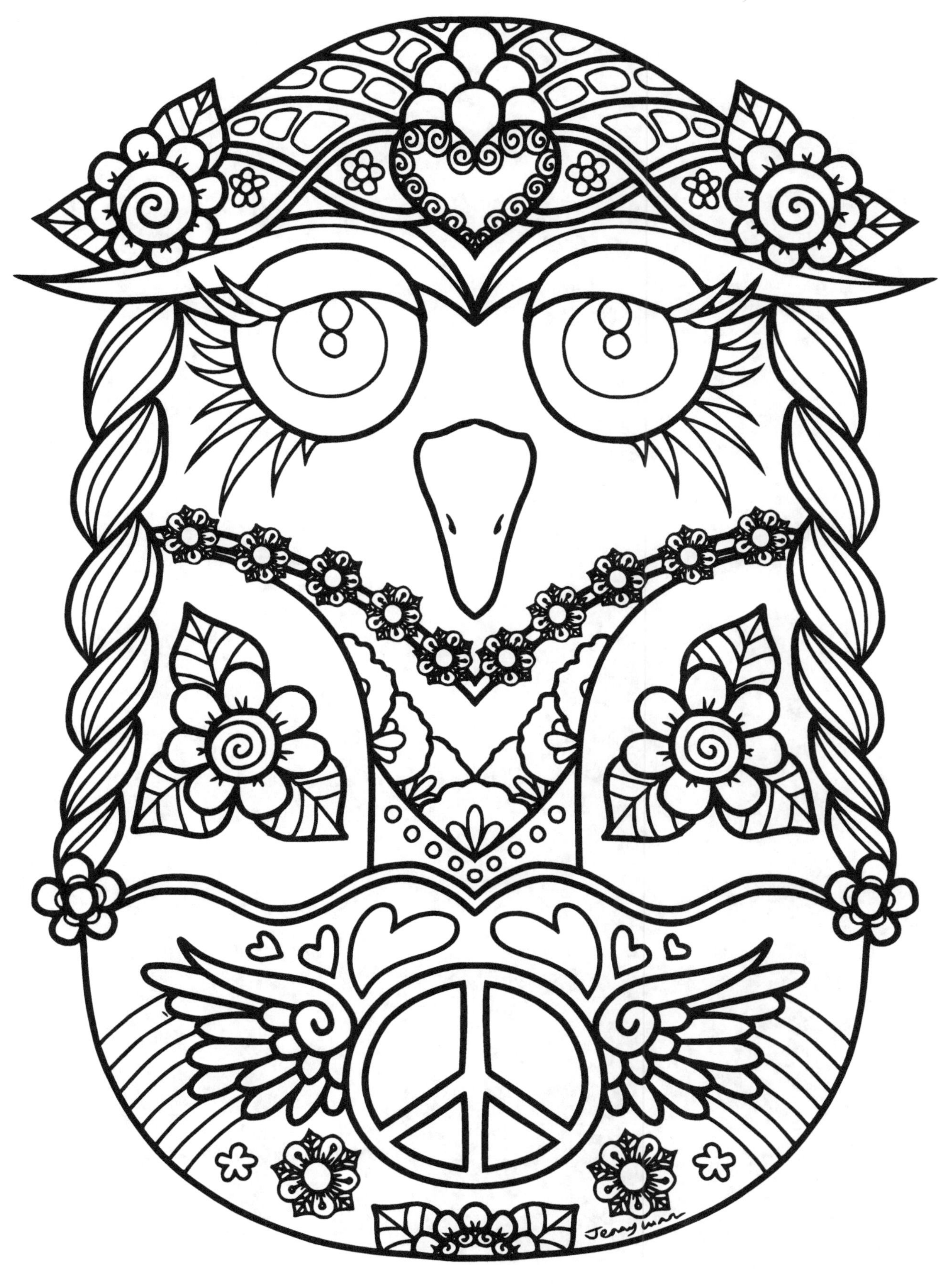

Whimsical Doodle Owl in the Egg by JennyLuan.com color by: ______________

Date:

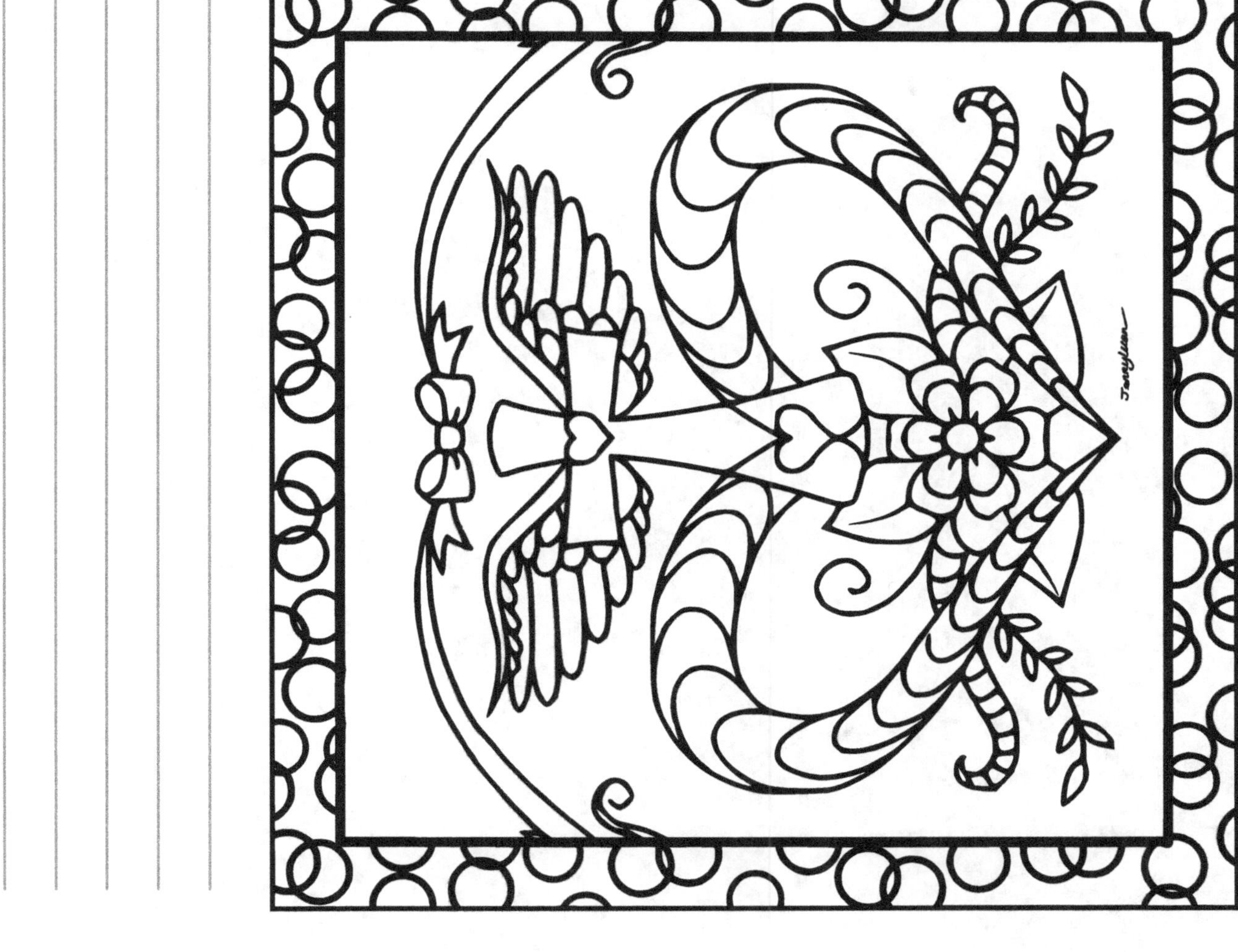

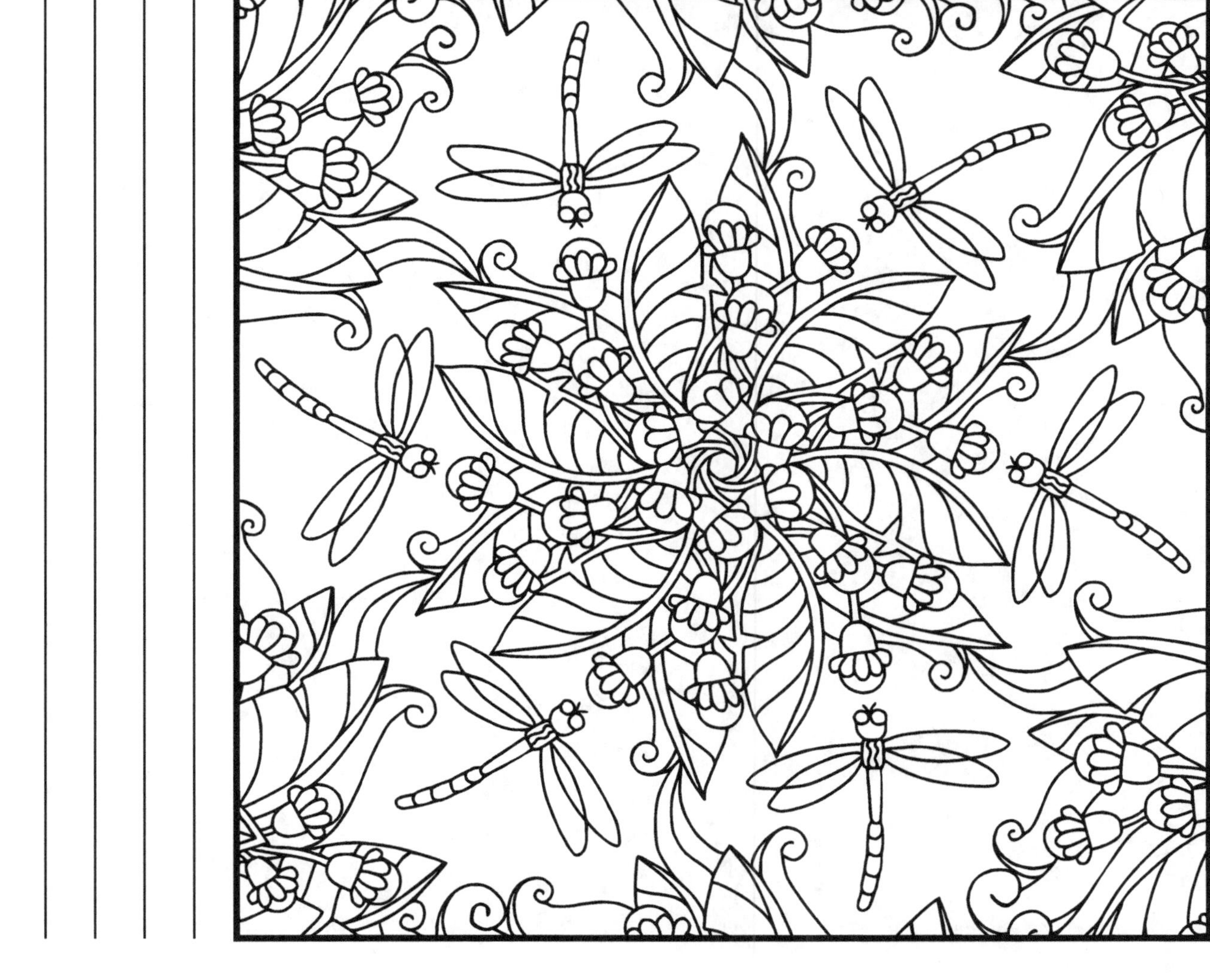

Whimsy Doodle Kaleidoscopes by JennyLuan.com   colored by:

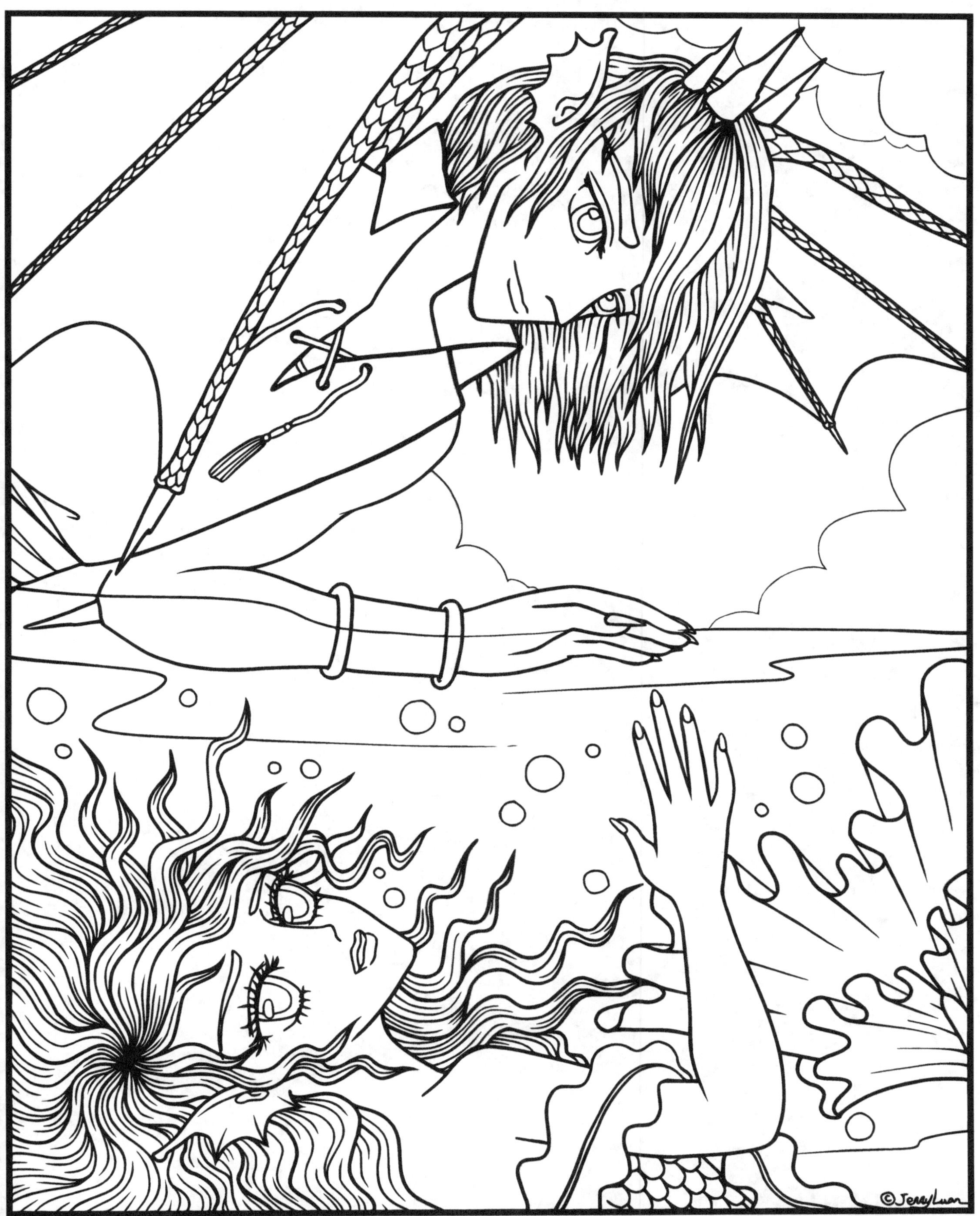

From Author:

A special thanks to my family who support my art. They are the main reason I wake up early and stay up late to create. I would also like to thank all those who support my art work.

Thank you to fans who visit my Facebook page, share, like, and leave comments. You may sign up for my monthly newsletter via my blog or Facebook page.

Please show me you enjoy my art and upload your coloring to my Facebook Page. I would love to see your work. I have albums for each book to serve as inspiration to other colorists and fans. facebook.com/InkTangleGifts/

You are also invited to join my Facebook group and share your coloring with me and inspire other coloring friends. https://www.facebook.com/groups/FanofJennyLuanInkTangleColoring/

Thank you again and if you enjoy this bundles, please leave a review.
xx
Jenny Luan

Social Media: #JennyLuanArt

* Newsletter: jennyluanart.blogspot.com/
* Facebook: www.facebook.com/InkTangleGifts/
* Instagram: @JennyLuanArt
* Twitter: @JennyLuanArt
* Pinterest: Pinterest.com/JennyLuanArt/
* Google Plus: +JennyLuanArt
* Website: http://www.jennyluan.com/
* YouTube: youtube.com/channel/JennyLuanArt

www.ingramcontent.com/pod-product-compliance
Lightning Source LLC
Chambersburg PA
CBHW081423250726
48654CB00013B/1784